Twentieth-Century Pessimism

and the American Dream

LEO M. FRANKLIN – 1870–1948

Twentieth-Century Pessimism and the American Dream

The Franklin Memorial Lectures, Volume VIII

Edited by RAYMOND C. MILLER

*Holder of the Leo M. Franklin Memorial Lectureship
in Human Relations at
Wayne State University for the year 1957–1958*

DETROIT—WAYNE STATE UNIVERSITY PRESS—1961

The lectures in this volume were broadcast locally by WDET (Wayne State University), nationally through the facilities of the National Association of Educational Broadcasters, and internationally by the Voice of America.

*The Leo M. Franklin Lectures
and the Occupants of the Leo M. Franklin Memorial Chair
in Human Relations at Wayne State University*

VOL. I   (1951)   TOWARD BETTER HUMAN RELATIONS

LLOYD ALLEN COOK *Professor of Educational Sociology*

VOL. II   (1952)   [OUR TROUBLES WITH DEFIANT YOUTH]
Unpublished

FRITZ REDL *Professor of Social Work*

VOL. III   (1953)   AMERICAN FOREIGN POLICY AND AMERICAN DEMOCRACY

ALFRED H. KELLY *Professor of History*

VOL. IV   (1954)   CONTEMPORARY PROBLEMS IN RELIGION

HAROLD A. BASILIUS *Professor of German*

VOL. V   (1955)   PROBLEMS OF POWER IN AMERICAN DEMOCRACY

ARTHUR KORNHAUSER *Professor of Psychology*

†VOL. VI   (1956)   THE CITY IN MID-CENTURY

H. WARREN DUNHAM *Professor of Sociology*

VOL. VII   (1957)   THE NATURE OF BEING HUMAN

MARIE I. RASEY *Professor of Educational Psychology*

† Out of print.   * To be published in 1961.

Titles of volumes differ in some instances from titles of lectures as originally announced.

Foreword

This volume comprises the eighth annual Leo M. Franklin Memorial Lectures presented at Wayne State University during the spring semester of 1957–58.

From 1899 to 1941 the late Leo M. Franklin served as rabbi of Temple Beth El in Detroit, and upon his death in 1948 his many friends there naturally sought to establish an appropriate memorial. Because Dr. Franklin's long career had been distinguished by his ecumenical interests and humanitarian concerns there was a strong desire for a memorial that would commemorate this phase of his life. Accordingly in 1950 Temple Beth El arranged with Wayne University—later to become Wayne State University—for the establishment of the Leo M. Franklin Memorial Lectureship in Human Relations, in the hope that from this lectureship would come new knowledge of the problems of human relations, new understanding of the forces which shape our relations with other men, new stimulus for cooperation in solving inter-group relations, and new resolve to face our individual responsibilities in carrying on the objectives to which Dr. Franklin devoted his life.

Each year a faculty committee carefully surveys the entire University faculty and recommends to the President a faculty member who has made a significant contribution to some important field of human relations. The President appoints this faculty member to the Franklin Memorial Lectureship for the following year and charges him with the responsibility for organizing a program of lectures on a significant phase of human relations and for involving three or four other persons of national stature in a co-ordinated lecture series. Naturally, this lectureship has come to be highly prized by the recipient and highly regarded by his colleagues in the University and in the academic community at large.

The Lecturer for this series, Professor Raymond C. Miller, is uniquely fitted to interpret a phase of human relations which was of intellectual and social concern to Dr. Franklin. They both lived in Detroit for a common quarter century, and as their paths repeatedly crossed they became friends. Both men came to understand well the constructive influences of the American dream upon the social and economic life of the nation during the nine-teenth century, and both observed with genuine concern the fading of this dream before the impact of the funda-mental pessimism of the twentieth century.

Dr. Miller's early life and education were in Kansas, while his graduate study in history was at the University of Chicago. Most of his long and distinguished academic career has been at Wayne State University, where he developed both basic and advanced courses in American history, guided the History Department during its forma-tive years, took a leading role in establishing the Graduate School and served in various administrative capacities. His research interests have tended increasingly towards eco-nomic and technological history and culminated in a recent book: *Kilowatts at Work: A History of the Detroit Edison Company* (1957). Beyond his academic achieve-ments Dr. Miller has devoted his talents to selected civic enterprises like the Detroit Historical Society and to the interpretation of issues vital to the diverse social and racial groups which comprise metropolitan Detroit.

Much of his thought has been given to the influence of peculiarly American ideals and optimism and to growing national pessimism in the wake of recent technological centralization and the new order of international relations. This is the theme of his introductory lecture and the frame of reference for the succeeding three lectures. Edward Littlejohn, a native of Australia and a young business executive, analyzes the significant effects of bigness and organization in American business and their impact upon our collectivist industrial society. Thomas C. Cochran, widely recognized authority in the field of business history, emphasizes the emergence of professional managers in the control of large corporations and their relationship to the evolution of the welfare state in America. Max Lerner, distinguished author and lecturer, interprets the importance of education, of intellectual freedom and of creativeness in the development of our contemporary popular culture. Together these four discourses constitute an important study in changing American values and attitudes.

WINFRED A. HARBISON
Vice President for
Academic Administration
Wayne State University

Contents

I

The End of the Age of Confidence
The Dream and our Heritage of Mistrust

RAYMOND C. MILLER

Professor of History
Wayne State University

The End of the Age of Confidence

THESE ARE critical days for us as a people. This is obvious to any observer, even the most obtuse. Nothing which will be said here will deny the obvious or attempt to minimize it.

What is significant, for purpose of this discussion, is not the peril as a reality, but the public awareness or consciousness of peril as a fact to which our lives must somehow be adjusted. This awareness is intrusive and almost completely pervasive. Our present self-analyzing preoccupation with choices and decisions—and the brooding consciousness that our actions may have unseen and unintended results—has tended to give to discussions of our national situation a confused, dogmatic, and hysterical shrillness, and has made our action stutter. The peril is not just an external fact; a part of our peril is our own reaction to the fact of peril.

Let me illustrate. A hundred years ago, while the telegraph was still a new and wondrous achievement, a group of adventurous men combined after a decade of work and heartbreaking disappointment to lay the first trans-Atlantic cable. The world rang with plaudits. Statesmen promised an era of international peace, resting on man's better understanding of his fellow man. Scientists pointed with pride to this latest achievement of their method, and with full confidence promised further revelations for the ultimate betterment of mankind and the achievement of society. The assumption was obvious, that

3

all such achievements would assuredly work together for good.

One hundred years later, Sputnik #1 was launched, and this time America panicked. This too was a superlative scientific achievement, a triumph over the unknown, a forward step in the march of science as epoch-making as had been the telegraph or the transoceanic cable.

The difference was in the reaction. Our universities beat their collective breasts, our scientists talked nonsense and were heard as if they were the new chief priests, politicians hastily shifted range in their barrage of denunciations, and journalists scared the rest of us to death with awesome diagrams and fearful prophecies. This time no one suggested that science was necessarily the bringer of all good, or that this step led inevitably to the road of human betterment; no one congratulated the Russians on their contribution to the world's scientific advancement and to a better world. A good deal of the history of the past hundred years is compressed in this changed reaction.

The fact of peril, international and domestic, will be from this moment assumed. My discussion will be devoted to the altered intellectual assumptions and presuppositions which may account for our sharply different reaction to these two events and which have shaped and conditioned our attitude toward this troubled world.

The words, "the American dream," are trite, but no other phrase quite so well includes that combination of anticipation and resolve which historically marked the nineteenth-century American as he faced his future. There is, of course, no national dream, and I am not trying to create an artificial composite soul. A dream is an intensely personal thing; each man shapes his own out of his own

4

nature and his own desires. The American dream is not the dream of America, but of individual Americans. The uniformity which makes it possible to refer to the American dream as a composite is the absence of any other kind of uniformity. We are the composite of all mankind, yet somehow distinguished from the rest of mankind by the nature of this combined anticipation and resolve which constitutes our national dream.

The American began by talking liberty. The theoretical defenses of individualism and individual freedom were worked out by philosophers of a dozen different countries. The American has seldom been concerned with the abstraction; it was his mission to reduce the idea to a commonplace by sheer reiteration. " We hold these truths to be self-evident—that all men are created equal." " Of the people, by the people, and for the people." " We, the people of the United States, in order to . . . secure the blessings of liberty to ourselves and our posterity. . . ." " Endowed by their Creator with certain unalienable rights . . . life, liberty and the pursuit of happiness." Every classroom in the land, every political hack on the hustings, every schoolboy orator at his class-day exercise, has echoed these patriotic phrases and has made them the vocal expression of a dream.

" Life, liberty, and the pursuit of happiness." I know all the saving reservations that it is the pursuit of happiness and not happiness itself which is guaranteed, but that distinction has no meaning. In our familiar usage, these are not two ideas, but merely two expressions of a single idea. Liberty gave to each man the right to define happiness in his own individual way, and then to pursue it as he chose, in any direction and by almost any method.

The sacred phrases of our patriotic liturgy thus gave

moral support to actions individually of the most diverse sort. To many good people, the result was a painful revelation and discovery, for free Americans did not always show themselves pure and selfless—though sometimes they did. In fact, they proved to be no better, and no worse, than anybody else. The colonial smuggler, defying King George's law, talked liberty even while his actions just skirted piracy, and he has had many successors through the decades since. The whiskey rebels of Pennsylvania, the illegal squatters on Indian land, the pre-emptor of public land, the speculator, the tycoon, the robber baron, these all pursued private purpose without external restraint.

America became a chaos of cross-purposes, and it is not surprising that visitors and native critics have alike been baffled at its contradictions and apparent formlessness, or that in our society they so often found the confirmation of their prejudgments of us. It is easy here to see what you choose to see. Americans have been dollar grubbers and sentimental philanthropists, patriots and pilferers, idealistic dreamers and, at the same time, crude materialists, honest men, and shysters unabashed and even proud.

Liberty meant the right of a man to define his own goals and purposes—to determine what happiness meant to him—and the right to pursue those goals with singleness of purpose as he would and could. Liberty, so defined, gave to our social order a tremendous dynamism, and in fortunate America the wealth of natural resources and the sweep of a new continent gave this dynamism room. In the economic field, as in every other area, the American dream allowed each individual to make what he could of himself, and to call any moves good which advanced him along his chosen path. Individualism itself became a value, even among individuals who themselves held the most diverse values.

It is a serious question, however, whether individualism is any more characteristic of America than is organization. From the Mayflower Compact, of sainted memory, to the almost identical vigilante committees which imposed their rule on lawless mining camps, the American has shown capacity and willingness to improvise and invent the instruments of a social order. The log rolling which created the frontier cabin, the voluntary discipline of the wagon train trailing across the prairies, the mutual interdependence for water in the arid West, the habitual cooperation of men, and women too, in farm and village life, these made life possible, or made it more full.

In time, the informality of a rural world matured in town and country alike into more formal organization: various denominations of the Protestant church; workers organized as the Knights of Labor; farmers—and their wives—who called themselves Patrons of Husbandry and met in Grange halls across the land; the Masons and a dozen other fraternal orders; the universal Grand Army of the Republic—to mention only the best known of their kind, and their number was legion. They sometimes provided entertainment in a society which was often grim, but the American seldom admitted that entertainment was his chief purpose. Instead, he proclaimed that his organizations were serious instruments by which he would improve himself and, even more commonly, his fellowmen—with or without their consent.

Men sought their own advancement through cooperation with others in tasks beyond the individual attainment, but this collective effort was something more than a mere enlightened selfishness. Man did not labor in the church merely to make his own election sure. The unanimity with which these organizations proclaimed their concern with the welfare of mankind, their frank and uninhibited resolve to improve society as a whole and the self-sacrifice which often marked their efforts, demonstrate that something more than an extended individualism was involved. Society was also a value.

The constantly used word "progress" was applied not so much to the altered position of the individual within society as to society itself. Not just man but mankind moved ever forward, and this advancement was a legitimate concern of man individually and of the institutions he devised, government included.

And as for the nation as a whole, what nineteenth-century American could doubt its beneficent future? The rolling oratory which proclaimed ours to be the land of freedom and liberty proclaimed that, for this reason, it was also the land marked for destiny. As the rest of the world inevitably advanced, benighted though it still was, it would show its enlightenment by patterning itself upon this most fortunate land. Invincible in war, perfect in institution, the home of the free (and the brave), America was great in her past, and was destined to be greater. In the eyes of her admirers, at home and abroad, America was not just another nation among many.

The United States (in the minds of its people) was unique, entrusted with a mission which marked it off from Europe—in spite of that continent's pretensions to a superior culture—and from the oriental tyrannies of the backward and immobile East. To the nineteenth century, America was the wave of the future; of this her own people were sure, and their certainty was confirmed as tens and hundreds of thousands of Europe's sons either sought for themselves and their children the boon of a homeland here or sought at home to shape their institutions and mold their lives on the American pattern, to match their steps to ours, and thus to progress. This was flattery indeed.

The American dream was, let me repeat, even in its nineteenth-century form complex and ill defined. It included individualism and a definition of human liberty which sometimes was just short of anarchy. But at the same time it included organization and the pursuit of a social purpose and, where necessary, accepted restraints by society, even the gentle intervention of the government when justified by a common need. And it included the assurance of a sure national destiny. There was no worry lest these elements prove incompatible, and no one doubted that the well-being of America and of all mankind would be advanced by the same means and in complete harmony.

I have used the word "dream," but I want to say again that this was neither a vague and vaporous abstraction nor a wistful and idle contemplation of a never-never land. The dream had meaning because it was firmly rooted in the belief of its automatic fulfillment. The end and the path were alike predestined. This was a form of determinism, and both America and the American awaited destiny with confidence.

It is difficult to tell when the nineteenth century closed, for its ideas and assumptions flowed easily past the century's turning point. In many ways, the first ten or fourteen years of the new century revealed aspects of the old with heightened clarity. Progressivism, proclaimed by the leadership of two great parties—or was it three?—found expression also in a dozen other fields of endeavor, both active and reflective, and called all good men and true to a new and glorious crusade. The nineteenth century closed, and the new one opened, in a blaze of optimism which made Utopia seem but a step away.

The literate figure of the century's end was likely to refer to himself as a liberal and thus to associate himself with a body of beliefs (and practices) which were the more unshakable because they were not recognized as beliefs, any more than the law of gravity was called a belief. His principles of law, economics and politics were held to be as scientific as mathematics and as firmly rooted in natural law, an inexorable law which was independent of man's will and beyond the direction of his institutions.

The progressive was a liberal who believed in individualism, in social progress, and in national destiny, but this progressive was something more than liberal, for he was not content to wait for the long slow process of evolution to work out its inevitable end; he was a good man in a hurry who proposed to give evolution a judicious push or two in the right direction. Mankind, by taking thought, proposed not only to add to its stature but also to speed up the growing process.

This was a heady idea, that man could shape his own destiny. The Utopias, with which romantics had long whiled away their idle moments, seemed suddenly attainable. The things man had sought, the aspirations he had voiced through the ages, seemed suddenly just a step away, a step which man had only to will to take.

To so enticing a prospect, few men or institutions could be completely indifferent. Many were profoundly altered. The church proclaimed the social gospel, the advancement of which became an added responsibility, and it sought the Kingdom of God on this earth. The school proclaimed progressive education and sought to shape the future as it shaped the young. The novelist and the dramatist each did his duty to society, as he sought to rouse mankind to exorcise its ancient evils, while reporters and journalists added their urging to these reforms.

In city and state, under lash of tongue and pen, man girded himself for battle against the forces of evil and prepared to correct those abuses he had too long tolerated. What was wrong with the world could be righted, if man would, and it was his job to do it. The ebullient Theodore Roosevelt and the bookish Woodrow Wilson gave voice not just to the desires of their following but to the hopes and dreams of the ages, grown somehow realizable in this glorious new day. And when Wilson led the nation into war, it was to accomplish that dream of the ages, the creation of a new international order of justice which would bring an end to war.

And now, from such high hopes, I move to pessimism. In this progression, I merely trace the path which the nation took in those first decades of the new century. Pessimism is not to be equated with despair. It does not imply that our state is hopeless or that our future individually or as a people is beyond redemption. There are prophets of gloom, on the campus and in the press, who loudly lament as disaster every change which has brought man out of his simple agrarian social order. Loud and nostalgic laments usually come from the city and from men who would undoubtedly refuse to go back to the farm. We, as a people, are going backward neither to the farm nor to the nineteenth century. There is no future in going backward.

Pessimism is not fatalism. As I use the word, it is simply the inversion of optimism. The nineteenth-century liberal believed that, unless something happened, all would work out well. The pessimist believes, and I think correctly, that in the absence of action things are just as likely to turn out wrong. We can no longer maintain the complacent view that that part of mankind which came to be this nation is an especially chosen people or that our people are in some fashion favored above all others. As with all mankind, our future is in our hands, and that is enough cause for pessimism.

One revelation which came with Progressivism was important, unforgettable; the very effort to control the social process launched the idea that it could be controlled, and, with that explosive idea, the safe, compact, harmonious, inexorable, self-regulating society of the nineteenth-century liberal world stood revealed as the fraudulent concept it was.

I am not foolish enough to suggest at this point that the nineteenth century had no problems or even that ours of the twentieth are more awesome. There is a dangerous historical distortion in perspective which makes the problems of the past, because we know the outcome, seem less foreboding than those of the present, on which we lack such foresight. It could even be that the nineteenth century, like a sleepwalker, was often in real peril but without the alarms and panic which would have prevailed if the danger had been seen. Because the nineteenth century believed that the outcome was automatic, there were no alternatives on means and no worry over choices of program or direction. Our generation has had no end of choices.

The earnest preachments of the Progressive may have

12

brought few changes to the political and social structure, but there is no doubt that World War I, the New Prosperity, the revolutionary New Era, the Depression, the New Deal, World War II, the Cold War have. Under pressure of a necessity which brooked no compromise, we made, in the social, political, and economic world, inventions and improvisions as daring and perhaps ultimately as dangerous as that which in the laboratory experiment produced the atom bomb. The most radical among the Progressives, urging on his fellow citizens a program of decision and reform, would have been appalled at action so extreme and at power so naked and complete.

There is no return to lost innocence. The techniques of direction and control, these social inventions which mobilized us for war and crises, will not be forgotten. Government has found the way to intrude with effectiveness in vast areas once forbidden to it. Here is mobilized power undreamed of, but it is not self-directing any more than the atom bomb is self-directing.

The American dream most emphatically did not deal with such things as techniques or instruments. The problem of purposes and objectives, that complex to which we give the name " values," is far more troublesome than means. The dream looked to the future, and because it did, it was concerned with these matters of purpose.

The American dream, ill-defined though it was, played an important role, for it served to guide present actions by checking them against a distant goal. It embraced individualism and talked liberty and the pursuit of happiness; it included a social purpose and called by the name " progress " the collective efforts of men to serve themselves and each other better through institutions of their own devising; and it affirmed a national destiny, exalted, un-

13

selfish, and thus the more sublime. The emotive words in which we dressed the dream pointed to the future—" pursuit of happiness," " progress," " destiny." For a long time, the American dream gave us our sense of direction.

In the twentieth century, this dream has come apart in our hands, and the ruined fragments cannot be restored. It broke, not from our carelessness, but from its own internal strain. Will you remember with me how the good people of the land, shocked at the inquity and corruption associated with the saloon and at the human distress and suffering attributed to the liquor traffic, joined hands to level it once and for all in universal Prohibition? It was an excellent illustration of a socially minded, humantarian move for human betterment. And will you remember the ardent appeals to liberty, which were vocally presented in that day of Prohibition, and the very odd places to which the pusuit of happiness took some Americans?

If Prohibition had been the only illustration of our new dilemma, we would be able to look back indulgently at that over optimistic generation. But it was not the first; it was only the most gaudy revelation, the most loudly debated illustration of the unresolvable conflict which has now become characteristic of our day.

Individual definition of ends and means, so long talked about as " liberty," clashed with society's decision to look to the common need. And on occasions, unfortunately frequent, both the individual and society found their objectives and traditional purposes to be contradictory to the positively asserted national interest. Traditional individualism and social progress proved often to be incompatible with each other and contradictory to the national interest. In the contention, the dream itself was fractured.

The American dream has split asunder, and we are in

14

the pathetic position of loving each fragment. We find ourselves no longer happily standing at Armageddon battling against unrighteous foes and massed wickedness. It is fun to battle for the right. Instead, we stand bewildered at a conflict in which right faces right, in which, by an odd convulsion of loyalties, we find ourselves enlisted in both armies so that we are at war with ourselves. It is no wonder that sometimes we show symptoms of a national split personality.

I voice your pessimism. There is nothing in the singing stars or the tides of time that guarantees the survival of America. Or, if she survives, there is nothing to guarantee that survival will not have cost what made the land unique. We face alternatives between success and disaster, and each success will only lead us to another decision.

We have talked a great deal about man's ability to rule himself. We have talked about democracy as a way of life, have boasted of it abroad, and have even turned it into a symbol emblazoned on our battleflag. Those were mere words, however sincerely used. We are about to try democracy at home, not a restricted democracy, but one equipped with power for good or ill as never was government before, prepared to make decisions about which there is no reservation and from which there is no escape anywhere in the social fabric. In the language of the day, here we go for broke. I hope you have faith in the democratic process.

We have been ill served in our day by the "lessons" which the nineteenth century so firmly impressed on our collective mind, the lessons which emphasized so strongly the nonvolitional that we came to doubt decision. They emphasized so strongly the functioning of a self-regulating

15

society and economy, with automatic built-in controls, that control or direction for any reasons except reasons of state left us timid. They emphasized so constantly the danger of interference with nature's law and natural processes that opprobrium and suspicion were reflected on any decision motivated by anything less than war and wartime need. The fears and self-doubts of a century now dead return to haunt us and, like ghosts, to distract us from the task at hand.

These things are true, and they have been said repeatedly, probably most often and most movingly by men of good intentions who are impatient at delay of their good works. The military leader worrying about defense in a threatening world, the socially minded humanitarian concerned with mankind's human tragedies, the planner seeking rationalized efficiency, the intellectual seeking for himself and his kind a new freedom and an improved opportunity, all these and a score of others use denunciations of the past as if they were bludgeons—and with them they belabor us and each other. The clamoring pressures of the present illustrate the difficulty of unending choice, sometimes even choice between one good and another. We could well wish for a return to the nineteenth century when the achievement of the dream seemed inevitable and when, with simple faith, we assumed that its several elements were harmonious and mutually compatible.

This we can no longer assume, but from the wreckage of the dream we can perhaps salvage those elements which made it the unique thing it was. I can hardly propose that we attempt consciously to create a new dream, for men find it difficult to worship a golden calf of their own conscious creation. To many people the suggestion that we cling to such an artificial construct, not because it is

16

true but because we need it, would appear to be indefensible and even impious. Perhaps we will not call it by the ancient, hackneyed name which the nineteenth century used, and for " dream " we will substitute another name for whatever will serve to give us again direction, coherence, and resolve.

Our historic dream raised to the level of values the individual, society, and the nation—all three important and cherished. From this moment onward, if these values survive it will be because we have willed them to. It is an awesome responsibility, and we will need our best wits. Involved is the survival of that which makes America's survival worth while.

In a second sense also, we have been ill served by our intellectual inheritance from the nineteenth century. The liberal of that century and his immediate heir, the Progressive of the first decade of the new century, for all their faith in the future, were vigilantly and aggressively alert lest anything or anybody obstruct our forward path. The future was sure, unless sinister forces intruded to corrupt us. As a people, we " viewed with alarm," loudly and often. That century left to us its specific collections of fears and prejudices which, like old wives' tales, have been passed on to succeeding generations.

The words " the robber barons," " the trust busters," " the wicked city " slipped into common usage and are expressive of the suspicion and distrust in which were held respectively the businessman class, the great corporation and the great city. The nineteenth century was persuaded that these new institutions, if I may use that word in so broad a sense, were incompatible with the survival of the values which America cherished. Thoughtful and public-spirited men viewed them with a fear which increased as these institutions became more pervasive.

The British tradition held government to be the business of gentlemen, either to the manner born or gentlemen by courtesy of the Queen, who bore the rule as an obligation and made of politics an honorable career. In our land also we had a tradition of aristocracy, though it was not quite like that of our British brothers, and it carried its weight of public responsibility. The planter South and the farmer West had sent their best sons to the service of the state, and there they had joined sons of the Adams family, the Lodges, the Roosevelts. It was this tradition of the gentleman and the scholar which, however imperfectly it was maintained, had held the general public confidence. This tradition was now being challenged. Our politicians seemed to be coming from another class, and, being in office, they showed a tendency to bow to the larger success and to be subservient to business leadership. Probably the dominance of the businessman and the subservience of the self-styled public servant have been exaggerated, but the term "robber baron" was at once a nineteenth-century reference to some kind of private interference in governmental function and an expression of a fundamental suspicion of businessmen as such.

The words "the robber barons" reflected a primary concern with the problem of men and leadership. The liberal liked to talk about the wall between business and government, but that wall in fact proved frighteningly penetrable. Evolution's law of survival, however fine it was in theory, brought to positions of command in business men whose special attainments, ethical standards, and concepts of responsibility left much to be desired, and yet bore proudly the very evident marks of success.

Let us say here that I think this picture of the " robber baron " is a caricature of the businessman, but the question before us just now is not its truth but the fact that public-spirited men believed that business developed character-istics and attitudes in its successful men which Americans were loath to see transferred to public life.

The second of the omnious trends of the turn of the century, which the otherwise optimistic generation also watched with concern, was the trend toward bigness in business institutions. This concern differs from the worry over the insights and values of the businessman, for it has to do with the institution itself. It would be easy at this spot to tangle ourselves in words. The corporation as a legal entity is old, and trusts are merely a form of fiscal organization, and monopoly has seldom been complete. These things have been said and said again. But the great corporation was, in hard fact, a new thing in the land. It thrust itself into a simple small-scale nineteenth-century industrial capitalism as rudely and as commandingly as when, in the Middle Ages, the rising town had shattered a social order built on feudalism. People may have used the words " trust " and " monopoly " inexactly, but they knew the social and public values they cherished, and they sensed in the great corporation an institution new in form, awesome in power, strange in behavior and perhaps incompatible with those values represented in the American dream.

The third shadow, that of the great city, hardly needs a definition. The myth of the farm and the farmer was firmly held. The husbandman, his feet planted in the soil of his own farm, was God's nobleman, endowed with simplicity and integrity and insight by virtue of his direct and unspoiled contacts with nature. In contrast, the city was artificial and tawdry; it paid excessive tribute to worldly success and demanded an excessive price for its pleasures. The city was sinful, and its children paid—to the third and fourth generation.

Even the sons of the farm who moved to the city shared the belief that somehow rural life was virtuous and the city suspect. Even they were alarmed by a population trend which, in the decades just before 1900, multiplied cities over the land which, by 1900, had half of America residing in town and city.

The things I have said are by way of preface to the lectures which follow in this series. I have suggested that the assumptions which served our nation well in the nineteenth century have left us with an unspoken fear of making decisions to face an age of continuing critical decision-making. The lectures will examine, in the light of a half-century of observation, the behavior of those institutions which aroused so much concern in the day of the muckraker. This is the timely and important task to which the series addresses itself.

In the past fifty years, the objects which caused alarm at the turn of the century have grown with the nation. The businessman and his expression of a business philosophy are more pervasive than ever, though sometimes the philosophy might sound odd to the robber baron. The big business corporations are more numerous and larger, though more urbane. And the big city has got bigger.

On the other hand, we would be hard off without them. The skill and administrative competence of the businessman, the superlative mobilizing instrument which is the great corporation, and the enormous potential which is the great city are a part of the national asset. At any rate, for good or ill, we have these, and we will not lose them.

The pessimism of our century stems not just from fear of our own competence and strength; we also doubt the tools with which we must work in this self-conscious effort of deliberate social creation. If, to attain our good ends, we must reshape or modify our institutional tools or establish unprecedented controls over them, it is time we found that out. If, on the other hand, these tools have been accommodated to the public good, then we do them wrong and ourselves injury if we handicap them (and thus ourselves) in these critical days. For we are now in an absurd position, with the businessman essential to us, and suspect; with the great corporation essential, and yet suspect; and with the city just suspect.

The Heirs of the Robber Barons

The Businessman's Role in Contemporary Society

EDWARD LITTLEJOHN

*Assistant Manager, Public Relations Department
Standard Oil Company (New Jersey)*

The Heirs of the Robber Barons

AT THE END of his well-known book, *The Epic of America*, James Truslow Adams speaks of the American dream as one of a land in which life should be better and richer and fuller for every man, with opportunity for each according to his ability. It looks to a social order of equality, that is, equality of opportunity regardless of the fortuitous circumstances of birth or position. It seeks not merely material plenty, though this has counted heavily. Rather, it promises the possibility of development to every man and woman, unhampered by the barriers of tradition or class. And, as Adams concludes, this promise has been realized more fully in actual life in the United States than anywhere else, though very imperfectly even among ourselves.

> Give me your tired, your poor,
> Your huddled masses yearning to breathe free,
> . . . .
> Send these, the homeless, tempest-tost to me,
> I lift my lamp beside the golden door!

In these famous words did Emma Lazarus give expression to American hopes. And today they have been repeated on the walls of the new terminal building at Idlewild as if they were equally relevant. But things are clearly different now. Indeed, even as Emma Lazarus wrote, the frontier as a continuous line of settlement was reaching its end. In 1903 her words were placed at the base of the Statue of Liberty, but the invitation they gave was a few years later to be radically restricted by the first of the Immigration acts affecting Europeans. Congress thus in fact proclaimed the closing of the frontier, but the United States, for those in possession and for the still sizable flow of immigrants, was still the land of opportunity.

When they reached the Golden Gate, Americans did not stop moving. There was still homesteading to be done in many regions, but more and more we turned from extensive to intensive development. Above all, commerce and industry that from colonial days had always been relatively important began to flourish greatly. At the turn of the present century the first large corporate structures appeared in railroads, steel, meat packing, oil, banking, farm implements, and so on. It was the age of the tycoons. Carnegie, Vanderbilt, Gould, Rockefeller, Harriman, Morgan, and many others, dominated the scene by individual energy and organizing ability, and, in some cases, not a little ruthlessness.

The conditions that produced these men have disappeared. Indeed, it would be difficult to accumulate similar fortunes. But the corporate form is now more than ever widespread. The big corporation has become the guiding institution of American life, but in the process its leadership has been transformed. Such is the complexity of contemporary economic life that no individual could singlehandedly direct a large corporation. Leadership must operate by integration and coordination. The function of top management is a unifying one. It is to make of separate specialties a group effort. The functions of the robber barons have been inherited by the chairmen of corporate committees.

There is, of course, in a sense, still a frontier. Though in the 1930's it seemed that the American economy had become static, we have in the past twenty years moved on again. New products, techniques, and services, such as television, plastics, jet propulsion, electronics, wonder drugs, air travel, motels—to name just a few—are evidence of the continuing momentum of American life. Beneath the surface, however, perhaps a more profound transformation has occurred, more profound, that is, than the invention of new products to amuse us or new conveniences to make our work lighter. It is, to be sure, only a continuation of trends to which I have already alluded. It has been called " the twentieth-century revolution," " the big change," " the managerial revolution." We are told we are now in a " new society," that we are participants in a " people's capitalism." The changes are not only organizational. With new patterns of organization have come new patterns of life and new attitudes of mind. The other-directed man, the organization man, it appears—not the pioneer, the cowboy, the farmer, the tycoon, not even the small businessman—is now the typical American.

There is currently a great ferment in social thought. Critics and commentators may differ in emphasis. They may disagree with one another. But the substance of the profound transformation they have described is not in doubt. And what does it amount to? It amounts to this: The United States, like the Soviet Union, like the United Kingdom, is becoming a collective society. In saying this I am not necessarily sounding an alarm. I am stating a fact. Individual enterprise is dead. It is dead, that is, if we mean by that phrase that American economic society is largely made up of businesses owned and managed by the same individuals. Our economic activities are in great part carried on by organizations. Most of these organizations are controlled by a group of managers, with the varying, but never very large, degree of participation of a board of directors whose composition for the most part is determined by existing directors, including especially those members of top management who are also members of the board.

Now no one is shocked by this, least of all the stockholder. He expects from his company good dividends and rising stock prices. And if he does not get these, he will be more likely to sell his shares than to attempt to unseat the management. Nor is the general public shocked by this. There is no widespread demand that more stockholders or that workers be brought into top management, far less that customers, or suppliers, or the community should elect the officers.

The top management, I have suggested, controls but does not own; but even that group does not operate without limitations. It usually must work through committees or at least through certain key individuals at lower levels. The pattern will vary in every corporation. The realities of power will be distributed among certain directors, the chairman, the president, the vice presidents, and in various degrees down the line. Length of service as well as ability will at times also count, but less so as the competitive struggle increases. So then, if the corporation is a piece of property, control over it (and therefore, in a real sense, ownership) is collective. It is variously apportioned on the basis of position, seniority, and, in rare cases, stock ownership, but usually control is spread far beyond those theoretically and legally in possession.

The interesting fact is that just as we are beginning to recognize the implications of the division between ownership and management—and I may say here they are still not recognized in many of the utterances of corporate management—a new and even more unexpected phase is emerging. In a recent study for the Fund for the Republic, Adolf Berle has drawn attention to the rapid growth of pension trusts. A pension trust, of course, is a different thing from an insurance trust. Whereas the insurance company must plan to meet obligations of a certain number of dollars at some point in the future, the pension trust fund must prepare to meet obligations which it is not possible to determine at this moment. In short, the insurance company need not worry about inflation; for a pension trust inflation is the crux of its problem.

As a result, pension trusts have been obliged to hedge against inflation by investing in equities. The equities of pension trust funds are at present running to thirty per cent of their assets, and maybe more. And Mr. Berle predicts the percentage may increase to forty or fifty per cent, including twenty to thirty per cent of the good equity stocks. In other words, an immense potential power of control will lie with the pension fund trustees who are responsible to no one, not even to those on whose behalf they administer the funds. Up to the present, pension trustees have not shown an inclination to use this power, but, generally, those that have power have been ultimately forced to use it.

This question deserves much further investigation and discussion, as Mr. Berle would be the first to admit. I mention it here only to emphasize again how far we have departed from the individual idea of property and enterprise. The main difference, indeed, as Mr. Berle points out, between the Russian or Socialist society and our own is the all important one of the philosophical content.

The collectivist trend of which I have spoken is not

29

confined to the corporation. Parallel developments have been going on in every part of American life. Just as great corporations dominate the field of industry, so large unions dominate the labor movement. The farmers are organized into three large farm organizations; the professions are represented by large professional associations, and similarly, trade associations, veterans organizations, chambers of commerce, and so on, reveal a pattern of powerful groups that amount, in fact, in Kenneth Boulding's phrase, to an organizational revolution. If, then, we are still to realize the American dream, clearly it must be in very different conditions, through very different institutions, and, indeed, in the persons of different types of men and women.

Despite these profound changes, there is a continuing and persistent thread in American life, at least in the past century, and that is the dominance of business activity and business values. As early as 1840, de Tocqueville commented that Americans carry their businesslike qualities and their trading passions even into agriculture as into their other pursuits. In the past century the growth and fluidity of American society have provided the continuing opportunity that is the American dream, and these qualities have been created and maintained by our business system. In a real sense, it is within our business system that most Americans have found their fulfillment in these last generations.

I am not suggesting that in this period there have not been times of trial and distress for our business society. In the thirties it seemed that the system had broken down—and for good. I remember well listening in the late thirties to the lectures of Professor Harold J. Laski at the London School of Economics and Political Science. For him, capi-

talist society was one of privilege. The fruits of industry
went to the few. Industry was organized for the benefit
of the ruling class. The only solution was for the state
to take over the means of production and administer them
for the benefit of all. He was not sure that this could be
done peacefully, for ruling classes never abdicate volun-
tarily. Indeed, to him, Nazism and Fascism were the
typical reaction of such classes when their privileges are
threatened.

In the United States socialism has been scored as im-
moral and inefficient. But these criticisms miss the point
entirely. In England, for example, the socialism of which
Laski was an exponent, began almost as an evangelical
movement. Men and women were socialists because they
were outraged by injustice. They were rebelling against
class privilege, against inequality and poverty. And in this
state of mind they could hardly have cared less about
questions of efficiency or about the future problems of
individual freedom in a growing bureaucracy.

In the United States the economy was for a time in even
worse shape, but there was no heritage of class bitterness
and, consequently, no strong attraction to socialist theory.
Americans did not turn to socialism, but they did turn to
government intervention. They did not want an ideal blue-
print that would make all things new. They demanded,
rather, correction of immediate evils. In Britain, socialism
made some inroads, but at the same time greater equality
was achieved. Nationalization brought, however, no cure
for economic ills. In the United States, likewise, government control was greatly extended, but on the whole with
beneficial results. And the economy eventually went forward to a new period of astonishing expansion. By way
of dividend, in our equal society there was even a shift to

greater equality with the proportionate rise in importance of a new consumer class of middle incomes.

I make this contrast between Britain and the United States in order to emphasize that, whereas business was under severe criticism in both countries, there was no strong movement in the United States to overthrow the economic system. The great majority of Americans retained the sense that something could be done and was being done. And now that decade of stagnation has been followed by twenty years of boom. If business was on trial in the thirties, it has been acquitted in the forties and fifties. The current recession does not alter this fact. In 1929 the total Gross National Product—the value of all goods and services produced—in constant (1947) dollars was 149 billion dollars. In 1941 it was 198 billion dollars. By 1956 it had reached 332 billion dollars. With this performance, with the jobs it is opening up, with the greater incomes it is providing, with the prestige it has regained, business is still the business of America.

The new roles of government and labor and other groups undoubtedly have limited the former dominance of business leaders. Their position, as I have suggested, was threatened by depression in the thirties and may be threatened again by future downturns and by the emergence of other and countervailing powers. But in the happier economic circumstances of the postwar boom business leadership is certainly more than ever asserted and accepted.

The businessman has a role which extends his influence beyond that implied by the word " business." It is not just a question of leadership in promoting economic growth. This, after all, is the primary function of businessmen. Nor is it only a question of the profound social changes that have come with, for example, the automobile or television. What I am referring to is the important fact that more and more our social and cultural institutions look to business for support. Large fortunes were once, and private foundations still are, important sources of support for social and cultural institutions. But now at a rapid rate business corporations and business foundations are becoming a major source of funds for hospitals, colleges and universities, art galleries, libraries, and the like.

And then there is the influence that comes from the social prestige of businessmen. It would hardly seem necessary to emphasize that business occupies an extremely large place in American life. And yet it is necessary. We accept the idea so fully that we fail to see its implications. The fact is that the dominance of business is a uniquely American phenomenon stemming from the special conditions obtaining here. Set apart from the Old World, rich in resources, with a growing, vigorous population, this continent provides in unique abundance the means of economic growth. The industrial revolution began in England, but in the United States, by reason of more abundant resources and the lack of historical obstacles, it was more complete. In many other countries, diplomats, writers, professors, civil servants, and editors occupy positions of the greatest influence. With us, the road to prestige is especially through leadership in business, and this in effect means more and more a top management position in a large corporation.

In the dark days of World War II, the great Italian historian, Guglielmo Ferrero searched for an answer to the disorder of the times. He found it in the principle of legitimacy. Whatever the type of government, it will be stable only if it is founded on the right to rule. " Of all human inequalities," Ferrero wrote, " none is as important in its effects or has greater need of logical justification than that established by power." [1] Whatever the principles of legitimacy—hereditary, democratic, aristocratic, economic, or a blend of them—the important point is that the public accept the system under which it is governed.

If we may apply this same principle to business, which in many ways does have the qualities of government, then on the whole the power and influence of business have been by and large accepted as legitimate in American society. Americans have found in business activity the road to advancement. Indeed, after a careful study of big business leaders in America, Warner and Abegglen concluded:

> The ordered process of occupational succession in Big Business demonstrates that at least in this prestigeful and highly valued part of our economic life our society is some-what more fluid and flexible than it was yesterday. There is more circulation in and out of the higher and lower statuses; more men from different family backgrounds enter, hold, and leave powerful positions. The fathers of the elite and the ambitious striving men at the bottom both have greater awareness that the principles of birth alone are insufficient for maintaining high status today. Values of achieved status and social mobility are expressed more fully, and those of inherited positions less so, than a generation ago.[2]

If imitation is the sincerest form of flattery, then Americans flatter business leaders. We have in large numbers continued to work in the belief that we are at the bottom only temporarily and that a desirable and possible goal of life is to replace those already at the top of the economic ladder.

I am not saying that business is always and everywhere

34

admired. From a number of angles it is constantly attacked. For one thing, business is suspect by reason of its power. This is not surprising. Those who are out in front are bound to get words of advice from the onlookers. A powerful nation, a dominant class, a large or successful organization whether of business or labor or baseball, is bound to attract criticism. Perhaps business is altogether too touchy. Those who have power must expect a running debate on their use of it, and ill-tempered blasts at radicals, eggheads, and socialists, far from refuting, are only too likely to confirm the idea that business is irresponsible.

Any discussion of businessmen in modern America must involve discussion too of the place of labor. If the business system is the road to power and influence, how is it possible to reconcile unions to this pattern? Do they in fact stand in contradiction to it? Undoubtedly, to a degree union bureaucracy offers an avenue to promotion competitive with management. It would, however, be too much to say that the labor movement seeks to secede from the economic system. Nor does it wish to take over. It is not dedicated to a Utopian political or economic theory. It is just another pressure group, and a most formidable one.

Like the farmer demanding price supports, the businessman arguing for a tariff, the congressman seeking federal funds for his district, the labor leader wants higher wages and more fringe benefits for his constituents. He sees management and labor equally as employees of the corporation. He does not wish to subvert the corporate system. He wants, in competition with management, stockholders, and consumers, to get as much out of it as possible. It is true that an important factor in the rise of the union movement was a sense of class. In joining a union the workers have seemed to accept their status as workers. They have sought not the escape of promotion to management, but greater benefits in their present position. Nevertheless, the majority of Americans still believe that they can move up, that the top places are open to all, and that at least through the generations there is the opportunity to progress.

There are differences of opinion over the degree of conflict that does exist between management and labor, and whether it is in fact transcended by acceptance of common social ends. On the whole I think we underestimate the strength of our American consensus, whether economic, political, or even racial. On this last point, the reaction of the Negro population to the demands by our society in World War II is illuminating. Despite the denial to the Negroes of important rights in American society, the stress of war did not shake their loyalty to the American community. How much more emphatically may we assert then that the conflicts between management and labor, while they are serious, do not put in question the fundamental principles of our social union.

An important reason why the class struggle does not exist to any great extent in this country is the variety of allegiances of workers. They are not only union men. They have also religious, political, and ethnic affiliations. Some are on the move economically. Some, that is, have the hope of material advancement. Most have a considerable degree of security in their jobs. Indeed, in winning greater security, unions have also tended to make themselves less necessary to their members. Whatever the cause in an individual case, workers in general do not commit their whole persons to either union or party as instruments of class warfare.

The labor movement is in a period of transition. The pulpit from which labor has in the past launched its criticisms is now somewhat shaky. It is clear that important reforms are needed. Just as corporations have been in the past under public scrutiny, so labor unions are now on trial. There is no doubt that some unions, as presently organized, threaten individual freedoms. The answer, of course, is not the destruction of unions, which would be neither possible nor desirable, but the enforcement of democratic procedures.

Beyond, however, the elimination of corruption and the broadening of union democracy is the question of the place of unions in our society. We have spoken of the legitimacy of the corporation. Upon what purpose, we may ask, do trade unions base their legitimacy? Twenty-five years ago there was need to redress the balance of power in the relationship between management and employees. But the days of the great crusade for unions of workers' own choosing are now past, and labor, it seems, has no other objective than more, and then more. Without suggesting that the details of a union contract are unimportant, I submit that such vast organizations, if they are to have legitimacy, must have purposes broader than victory at the bargaining table and proportionate to their impact on the total economy.

In our time we have seen emerge three great centers of power—the state, large corporations, and big labor. They must be recognized for what they are, as the natural outgrowth of a technological revolution. In order to enjoy the benefits of industrial society, we have had to pay the price in large-scale organization. But we are fortunate that we have in fact developed a pluralistic society in which, if individual does not balance individual, at least by and large, great power concentrations are balanced by other centers of public and private power.

I do not take a pessimistic view of our future. Admittedly, the problems we face in respect to individual freedom in a world of organizations are immense. But they are no greater than the problems we have faced and resolved in the past quarter of a century. So far as business and labor are concerned, what is needed for further progress is frank acceptance of the realities of recent economic history. Neither can afford to continue as if their bargaining concerned only themselves. Each must rise beyond the limited philosophy of individual enterprise and union solidarity to a vision adequate to the needs of a collectivist industrial society.

A lot of nonsense is written about the American way of life and the forces seeking to subvert it. We might be spared much of this alarmist and oversimplified comment if its writers would study history—the history particularly of social revolutions. As a rule, demands for social change stem not from the conspiracy of the few, but from the discontent of the many. Conspirators may use discontent for their own ends, but they must first have the revolutionary situation.

It is true that in our day we have seen, as in Czechoslovakia, sudden subversion, but there we have what in effect was foreign conquest rather than domestic revolution. The causes of revolution, whether peaceful or otherwise, are always complex; but essential among them are discontent and the belief that there is a remedy. Such a revolutionary situation does not now exist in the United

States, and, despite the alarums of the late Senator McCarthy, it did not exist in the past decade.

We are not threatened by subversion, but it is sometimes suggested that a more fundamental division is appearing in our society. The time is coming, it is said, when the parties will divide themselves more strictly into two political camps—on the one hand, conservative, and on the other, labor and liberal. Such talk is, of course, not new. If, however, the division takes place—and I do not believe it will—then a fundamental premise of American democracy and the American economic system will have been dropped. Those who are winning will have called off the game. At that point we would expect the great debate concerning the legitimacy of the economic system to begin in earnest, and on the dangerous ground of class distinction. Evidently, too, the position of businessmen will have considerably deteriorated because the lines will be drawn not between business and a part of organized labor, as is sometimes now the case, but between business and, so to speak, an official political opposition.

America is a loose knit country. This is the price and also the safeguard of unity. Our political system is successful because it generally does not permit any issues to be pushed to a dangerous point. Under the tighter British system, a cabinet with a majority in Parliament is limited only by the internal check of British restraint and at last resort by the threat of violence. Our social, economic, and geographical variety requires a more flexible political structure, but its flexibility is also its strength. We can understand why those who are devoted to ideological purity long for a vehicle to express it. But they should remember that in excluding difference and dissent they would also narrow the base of their support. Realism in politics

39

demands that we steer between rigidity and flexibility—the rigidity that leads to splinter parties and the flexibility that compromises effective action.

I have mentioned the needs of a collectivist society. What are some of these needs? Among them is a more energetic search for principles of unity between management and labor within the corporate enterprise and, indeed, among all employees. In the past twenty years unions have been a divisive force. They grew in a struggle against management. But their crusading purposes have now largely been achieved. Unions are no longer growing. In fact in the last five years the proportion of union members in the work force has actually declined. More important perhaps is the rise in relative importance of salaried workers who show little inclination to become part of organized labor. In the fifteen largest corporations in the country the salaried work force amounts to one-third to one-half of the hourly paid production force.

Where then does labor go from here? For the workers' need will be not so much representation against but integration in the corporation. I do not have in mind profit sharing. To this end of greater partnership, profit sharing, it seems to me, would contribute hardly at all. When profits are earned, profit sharing gives workers a bonus at the *end* of the year. It does not necessarily increase their sense of participation in their *daily* work. Nor does it create any greater degree of social partnership. And the same may be said of socialism. Despite the high hopes in Britain that nationalization would give to workers a sense of service to the public rather than to private profit, the reality has been the exchange of one boss for another.

The problem of restoring to the worker a greater sense

of the significance of what he is doing with eight hours of his day is not easy. There have been many interesting experiments, such as the Nunn-Bush plan of production sharing and the incentive system of the Lincoln Electric Company. There is the John Lewis partnership in Britain, and the pioneering Carl Zeiss foundation in Germany. And yet these plans, while interesting, amount to merely a drop in the bucket. In view of the magnitude of the task, there is in fact very little thought being given to ways and means of increasing the satisfaction of factory work.

In the industrial revolution, forces were introduced which were to carry man from one world to another. With automation these forces are to become more pervasive than ever, both geographically and perhaps also in their effect on human personality. There is no need here to expatiate on the effects of the continuing industrial revolution. It has brought immense benefits. It has brought also serious problems. On the debit side is the acute loneliness of man in the modern world. Nowhere does he fully belong. An employee is not a whole man, nor is a consumer. No more is a suburbanite or a voter. Religion places man in perspective, but it is no longer the central point of our lives. To each place we take a part of ourselves, but nowhere our whole personality. The rise of democracy has added a new potential to the development of every man. The industrial revolution has offered, and in some degree fulfilled, the promise of the abolition of degrading poverty. But a price has been paid. The machine has multiplied man's powers; it has also imposed upon him the burden of its discipline.

I am speaking, of course, of problems to which there are no easy answers. They are rooted in the nature of our civilization, and, I might add, some believe they may

41

be the death of it. As one follows the day-to-day debate on the problems of the economy in the press and in the publications of unions, corporations, and chambers of commerce, one sometimes has the impression that in the long run much of it is irrelevant and that our energies are dissipated in attacking superficial issues while the decisive ones lie unobserved beneath the surface.

Recently, in a symposium organized by the Committee for Economic Development, a group of distinguished thinkers of the free world were invited to comment on the question, " What is the most important economic problem to be faced by the United States in the next twenty years? " In his reply, Professor Roy Harrod, of Christ Church, Oxford, termed as fallacious the argument that the needs or desires of men are unlimited and that there is no satiation point. It is only, he said, for a small highly educated minority that there is no satiation point. With the economic problem being so nearly solved, there will re-emerge for Americans in these next twenty years the question—no less—what is the purpose of man's existence on this globe?

The economic problem is close to being solved in the United States, if it is not in the world at large. We may now therefore begin to be plagued by insistent questions as to the purpose of our " busyness." As we have seen, the conditions of American history and geography have permitted and indeed encouraged the business virtues. The American people have on the whole had what they wanted. We have directed our attention especially to the fulfillment of man's desires as a consumer, and, in satisfying him, the businessman has reaped his reward. We have been more concerned with the technical apparatus of society than with creations of beauty and of pure thought. St. Augus-

tine once said that an architect builds a durable house
with the aid of temporary scaffolding. The technical
apparatus is that scaffold. It will only serve us if it permits
human personality to grow richly within it. As a people
we are not, on the whole, curious about philosophical
considerations, about forming general ideas as to why we
work and live as we do. Better than most peoples, we face
and solve our problems, but can we explain by what
principles we have acted? It is true we refer constantly
to the American way of life, free enterprise, and the like.
But after half a century of use economic change has
emptied these concepts of all meaning.

And so it is we have only the vaguest ideas about the
corporation, and they are often incorrect. Who owns it?
Who controls it? How do workers, management, stockholders, the community, stand in relation to it? Above all,
how may it accomplish ever more fully the purposes of a
democratic society? This is the heart of our industrial and
indeed social problem—so to organize our economic institutions that all can accept and work toward shared objectives.
Plato, Aristotle, and the long succeeding line of political
thinkers, have reflected on the nature of justice, citizen-
ship, power, authority, and the like. In our modern world,
these concepts are no less relevant; but they are relevant to
the corporation as an economic community as well as to
the state as a whole.

We hear much of the moral crisis of our times. There
is, as we now realize, also an intellectual crisis. It is not,
however, only in the area of science; it exists too in the
world of business and labor. There is, as I have suggested
earlier, a ferment in social thought. This ferment has not
yet penetrated deeply the business world. Business in the
twentieth century is no longer the sum total of a variety of

private arrangements. At least the managers of the larger corporations and unions have powers of decisive political and social importance. It is then urgent that they think and understand our times as well as act in them.

A lack of philosophical spirit is above all a handicap in our foreign relations. Our economic and social practice is far ahead of our theory. "Capitalism," after all, is a bad word to most of the world, and "free enterprise" has the flavor of more rugged days. Those who have visited the United States know the reality through experience, but what of the millions who will never see these shores? Communism has been poor in performance, but its theory has moved mountains. The shams of Communism, Barbara Ward has said, come clothed in the language of poetry and hope. Their power, she asserts, is in the echoes they stir deep in men's hearts. To their impact, what is our answer? It cannot be in statistics, whether of incomes, TV sets, or automobiles. The complicated but impressive facts of American life cannot be effectively communicated. Only ideas can defeat ideas. Only ideas can carry around the world the hope of American achievement.

America was promises which brought men hurrying to these shores. America is promises, but what are they? The job routines, the pale contentment of suburbia, the ball games, the movies and magazines? Clearly not. But is there a faith and purpose that gives them life? Inarticulate ourselves, we turn to our forefathers. In those great documents, the Declaration of Independence, the Bill of Rights, the Federalist Papers, is our faith. Those documents, however, grew out of the context of their times and they must be rethought in the context of ours. How do they apply? How should they be applied to the organizational revolution of these times, to the problems of the big corporation, the big union, big government? How to the achievement of international order, of which we stand so much in need? The Federalist Papers are among the great achievements of the human intellect. Who shall write a new series of Federalist Papers, not to deplore the present, but to discover in it the elusive paths to a continuing and ordered liberty?

Up to this point I have spoken mainly of the changing face of America at home. It is important that we address ourselves in more detail to new conditions abroad. If in the past America has been motivated by dreams, they were dreams that could find fulfillment in the rich resources of this continent. Throughout our history, by and large, we have retained control over our destiny; we could live our lives largely within our own borders. Today, the conditions determining our life are increasingly external.

At the mid-point of the twentieth century, the framework of American life is global. We are no longer in a position to watch the affairs of the world and intervene as and when we see fit. Indeed, whereas in the past the world looked to America as a haven from domestic tyranny and European wars, now Europeans are inclined to act on the assumption that they might, if they wished, be neutral and let the intercontinental ballistics missiles whistle overhead.

Americans, at least young Americans, are apparently not too worried by these global threats. If we are to judge by the surveys, college students' hearts are set on a good job in a large organization, a ranch-type home in the suburbs, a beautiful wife, two cars, and at least $15,000 a year. It is, however, difficult to reconcile this current edition of the American dream with the century of missile warfare. The American dream was founded on America as a haven—a haven, that is, where a man could start afresh. By the inexorable forces of history, that haven is now the command post in a global struggle. Our energies and our resources gave us wealth. They gave us also power. We might have hoped that this power would be simply added protection for the continuing fulfillment of our dreams. But power, unfortunately, cannot be bottled. It is an act of force. It creates action and reaction. Unused, it leaves a vacuum that something else will fill. Indeed, the mere existence of a power center seems to provoke a threatening response.

The question before us is whether in our business society today we can find continuing fulfillment of the American dream. It is true, as we have seen, that America considered in isolation was and, I believe, still is promises. The fruits of American energy and American resources are still the envy of the world. Such a question, however, can no longer be asked in an American context. The good life for Americans is now inextricably tied to peace and progress throughout the world. And we may indeed have cause for twentieth-century pessimism unless this challenge is met.

As President Eisenhower said in his recent State of the Union message, our long-range problem is not the stamina of our enormous engine of production. It is to bring our immense resources to bear confidently and creatively both here and in the whole free world. And it is not just a quesion of economic resources. The Soviet Union is pressing into the service of its expansion every human activity—trade, economic development, military power, science, research, the arts, education, and not least, the ideas and principles by which it lives.

The problem was dramatically stated by Professor Denis Brogan of Cambridge University. "For the first time," he wrote,

> I share, not the hostile emotions of the European intellectuals but some, at any rate, of their fears [for the United States]. . . . For the first time in my thirty years' study of the American way of life, I am not convinced that it, at the moment, has what it takes to win this contest. I am convinced that it will prove not to have it if there is not a very fundamental stocktaking that will involve the abandoning of some comforting illusions and, indeed, of some totally justified beliefs that were true, relevant, and comforting only yesterday.[3]

Among the attitudes he proposes for reconsideration are particularly the American "pragmatic" attitude to education and the American's reverence for the businessman not *in* business but outside it. On the question of education, let me no more than echo Professor Brogan's assertions that if our aim is to give everyone a college education, then the quality of that education is bound to be low, and that it is time we acquired an "undemocratic bias" in favor of brains.

His comments on the second attitude are more directly relevant here. Mr. Brogan's thesis is that the qualities of a businessman are not those that fit him for politics. As a supplier of hardware he is unrivaled. But as the judge of what hardware is needed, how it is to be used, and what the final choices are to be, he is no better a judge than anybody else. And the fact that "he has met a payroll" is neither here nor there. For the great issues of policy, of strategy, of the great political "art of the possible," require other talents than those developed in the relatively predictable and rational world of business, where the solvency of the firm is necessarily the guiding consideration.

This is a powerful indictment indeed. It is not new, however. As far back as 1913, Brooks Adams concluded his book, *The Theory of Social Revolutions*, with these words:

> It is hard to resist the persuasion that unless capital can, in the immediate future, generate an intellectual energy, beyond the sphere of its specialized calling, very much in excess of any intellectual energy of which it has hitherto given promise, and unless it can besides rise to an appreciation of diverse social conditions, as well as to a level of political sagacity far higher than it has attained within recent years, its relative power in the community must decline.[4]

And yet almost half a century later, capital, as Adams calls it, or business, as does Brogan, maintains its position in American life. I believe it will continue to do so in the future. Business will continue to be the major ingredient of the American way of life, insofar as we continue to be faced with the problems of the organization of vast resources, human and material.

Though the American dream implied a decisive break with the past, we pay great deference to our own historical traditions, at least to those of the founders of the republic. Indeed, Jefferson felt it necessary to warn us against those who ascribe to the preceding age a wisdom more than human, who look at constitutions with sanctimonious reverence and deem them like the ark of the covenant, too sacred to be touched. In fact, however, we have never allowed reverence for the Constitution and the Fathers who made it to stand long in the way of change. Americans have been an adaptable people. We have had to be in order to meet the problems of a new country, and we have continued to adapt ourselves to the technological changes our own ingenuity has brought about. Adams predicted that capital would abandon the contest and relinquish its place of influence, instead of which it was transformed and a capitalist society became a managerial society. Brogan is alarmed at the inflexibility of business practice in the presence of the new, the unknown, and the uneconomic. In the light of the past, it is at least likely that new conditions will remake our business institutions and develop new types of business leaders. Certainly we are in a period when the survival of the United States is in danger. But by the same token there is every reason to expect that business leaders will emerge who are aware of the things that the nation needs and can bring their business operations into a constructive relation to them.

Far-reaching changes have already taken place in our business society, as Frederick Lewis Allen pointed out in *The Big Change*. America is crammed from end to end with private organizations and associations—national, state, and local—designed to look out for one aspect or another of the common good. In most of these, businessmen play active and often leading roles. This development is an aspect of American life that we perhaps take for granted but that astonishes the Europeans. It would also have astonished our grandfathers. If American businessmen have moved aggressively into the vital field of community service, which may be related, but certainly not directly related, to the profit-and-loss statement, I see even more reason for them to respond to a challenge in which no less is at stake than the survival of their country.

The mistake of Brooks Adams and Denis Brogan is

that they in some way separate businessmen from other Americans. The virtues and even the shortcomings of businessmen are not unique to them but are in varying degrees shared by all Americans. The conditions that have produced businessmen and brought them to leadership in this country have also made their decisive mark on politicians, editors, labor leaders, teachers, writers, clergymen, and every one of us. We must not fall into the fallacy of thinking of the business world in abstraction from the rest of the community.

Moreover, businessmen themselves are only the current tenants in the great industrial and commercial organizations they manage. In Pareto's doctrine of "the circulation of elites," the dominant class, as he terms it, is continually experiencing dissolution and yielding to a new class that rises from the people. Though one may not accept Pareto's views in detail, it is clear that there is in America a continuing circulation from and to the top management group. The thesis that businessmen form an exclusive ruling class falls before the record of social mobility. To be sure, they have power, but those that exercise it are recruited from the entire social system. This is not to say that men can go from the bottom to the top in one generation, but there is a good deal of upward movement at every level. It is by this process that American industry has found the leaders for its vast business organizations. It is by this process, too, that America will find the leaders for the political tasks it now faces.

For better or worse, we are entering a political age, one in which issues of state will dominate our lives. We hear many warnings about the danger of strengthening government at the expense of weakening the private sectors of society. Certainly the traditional American concept of liberty against government has been weakened by the developments of the last decades. But the dogmas of private enterprise and union solidarity are of little value in the conditions that confront us. The state has grown in power because that power was necessary to fight wars, both hot and cold, to combat inflation, to maintain full employment, and to do other things which our society needs. The corporation has grown in size because only such an economic instrument can provide the greater abundance of things Americans want. And labor and agriculture have built their power too on the solid base of the interests and needs of their constituencies.

We are today faced with the task of creating from a chaos of competing power systems, both at home and abroad, an organic and stable social life. Not rising productivity, important though it may be to many countries, but the creation of new political and social relationships is the major problem. At home the question is how to control and harness for good our new world of large organizations, and abroad, how to create political and economic institutions to express the common purposes of the free world.

In this task we will need both doers and thinkers. We will need organizing capacity and philosophic vision. Without the former we can do little; without the latter we may do much but to no purpose. And, insofar as businessmen play the major role in the American community, they have a particular responsibility to recognize and respond to its needs. " Until philosophers are kings, or kings and princes of this world have the spirit and power of philosophy, and political questions and wisdom meet in one . . . cities will never have respite from their evils,—no, nor the human race. . . ." These famous words of Plato express perhaps a forlorn hope; indeed, they might be matter for cynical humor. Yet the ages best remembered are those in which great thought and great action were rightly blended.

The business leaders of the early years of the century may or may not have been rightly termed robber barons, though some did indeed carve out feudal economic empires. The leaders of today cannot claim ownership of their corporate estates, but the effects of their decisions extend throughout the nation and beyond. In the more rugged days of our economic development, the tycoons, as Professor Allan Nevins has reminded us, did much for America. Today their heirs may do the same, but it will be in the tradition not of the robber barons but of the philosopher kings.

The Sons of the Trust Busters

The Corporation and the American Dream

THOMAS C. COCHRAN

*Professor of the History of
the People of the United States
University of Pennsylvania*

The Sons of the Trust Busters *

ON SEPTEMBER 13, 1899 the Chicago Civic Association assembled a meeting of 700 American leaders to discuss the menacing problem of the trusts. National political leaders, state governors, journalists, academicians, and representatives of commercial, industrial, and labor organizations attended. The great popular orator, W. Bourke Cockran, spoke at length, maintaining that some combinations were beneficial because they " cheapen commodities." He was answered by William Jennings Bryan, who proclaimed that " there can be no good monopoly in private hands until the Almighty sends us angels to preside over the monopoly. There may be a despot who is better than another despot, but there is no good despotism." [1]

This large assembly with its wide press coverage was just one indication of how apprehensively people at the turn of the century regarded the impact of the large semi-monopolistic corporation on the traditional values of American life, on what we are here terming the American dream. Similar illustrations may be found in all spheres of contemporary thought. President Theodore Roosevelt devoted a substantial part of his first message to Congress to a cautious evalution of the trust situation. That his antitrust position was regarded by many as too moderate, because he was not promising to demolish this new threat to the American way of life, is shown in the comment

* Parts of this paper have been published in *Pennsylvania History* for January, 1957, and are reproduced by permission.

made by the popular humorist, Finley Peter Dunne, speaking through his famous character Mr. Dooley:

> " Th' thrusts are heejus monsthers built
> up be th' inligtened intherprise iv th'
> men that have done so much to advance
> progress in our beloved country," he says.
> " On wan hand I wud stamp thim undher fut;
> on th' other hand not so fast." [2]

But, in spite of the President's somewhat equivocal attitude toward big businessmen, his attorney general's office instituted forty-five antitrust prosecutions, and his rather conservative successor, William Howard Taft, gave his approval to ninety such proceedings.

What was the substance of this American dream that appeared to be menaced by the trusts? The dream was a set of themes or values that appeared to offer unique promise in American life. Democracy, equality of opportunity, individual responsibility and achievement, the right to pursue one's happiness or betterment without interference, and financial success as a reward for frugality and hard work were basic to the substance of the dream. If the monopolists were really closing off the avenues to successful individual enterprise, they were endangering all of these values.

The facts of the situation between 1897 and 1904 gave reason for alarm. At the end of the depression in 1897 there had been only about a dozen manufacturing companies with over twenty-five million in capital; by 1904 there were forty such companies. In addition, public utilities and railroads were becoming larger and all big companies were increasingly influenced by a few great banking houses. If this rate of growth were to continue, it was reasoned, American industrial activity would before long come to be controlled by a hundred great corporations, or even by a single small syndicate of bankers and industrialists.

Men of the day feared that the American dream of widespread opportunity for a young man to succeed in his own independent business was becoming unrealistic. " Optimists in the nineteenth century, and self-made men most of all, had taken opportunity for granted. But men coming to maturity in the early twentieth century were less sanguine about their prospects." [3] It was and has subsequently been widely supposed that the areas open to small business were diminishing and that in the future able entrepreneurs would have to be satisfied with managerial posts in great enterprises. In 1902 an extreme pessimist, W. J. Ghent, wrote an article entited " The Next Step: A Benevolent Feudalism," in which he forecast a fascist type of state controlled by corporate business leadership.[4]

Let us see what in fact did happen and what the actual changes have meant for business leadership in American society and for the values implied in the American dream.

But first let us make clear what did *not* happen. Three basic sets of factors go far to explain why big business did not eliminate small and become the rule in American life.

In the first place, in most types of business activity gigantism has not proved profitable. Only where the needs of technology demand a large fixed capital, as in railroads, public utilities, and certain types of manfacturing, have big companies been able to eliminate all small competitors. But changes in technology continuously open new types of manufacturing activity to alert entrepreneurs. Moreover, the chief opportunities for independent operators, whether in 1800, 1900 or 1958, have always been in the main areas of business: wholesale or retail trade, brokerage, and service. In these areas large companies have been rare. By 1904 bigness and monopoly in manufacturing had pretty well occupied their place in a mature industrialism. In the succeeding years monopoly declined and the business areas occupied by very big firms did not greatly increase.

In the second place, the business community as a whole has experienced an enormous and continuous growth. The number of all types of business enterprises has steadily risen in relation to the total population. In 1900 a nation of seventy-five million people had about a million and a quarter separate firms; by 1950 the population had doubled, but the number of firms had increased over three-fold. This increase in the proportion of Americans who realized their dream of being independent operators has come from the great growth of those sectors of the economy, such as free professional activity, trade, and service, in which small enterprise has been the rule. The increase has also been stimulated by the shift from farming to business. Though I do not wish to imply any literal transfer, it is interesting to note that entrepreneurs for the almost three million new business firms could have been supplied from men squeezed out of agriculture.

In the third place, continuing public support of anti-trust activity has helped prevent the monopolists from gaining control of the economic system. At one time or another over the last sixty years the leaders of almost all of the manufacturing giants have been warned by the government that further conquest of their market by elimi-nation of competitors would involve prosecution. As a result, in the big-company areas monopolistic competition rather than monopoly became the rule, and in many cases small competitors lived comfortably under the price umbrella maintained by the giants, while developing smaller-scale specialties that were unprofitable for the mass-production lines of the big companies.

The monopoly economy which was feared did not, then, become a fact. American business can still be viewed as divided by a vague line into two unequal parts, which, with dangerous oversimplification, can be called big and little business. Our general preoccupation with big business and its social implications ought not to lead us to ignore the dynamic, aggressive, individualistic, competitive small business which is not declining in twentieth-century America. In the discussion which follows, most of which deals with the causes and consequences of bigness, the other part of the economy must not be forgotten, even if reference to it is not repeated.

Although the last fifty years have not produced or even increased monopoly, they have brought forth two great changes in our social system which in a larger perspective will prove to be epoch-making. The first is the rise of a new conception of the socio-economic role of government which, for convenience, can be called the " welfare state." The other is the evolution of what I choose to call " managerial enterprise " in the large companies. For observers in the year 2000, these changes may seem as important as the end of feudalism, the rise of world trade, or the beginning of industrialism.

Managerial enterprise and the welfare state, while differing in historical beginnings, have exercised strong accelerating pressures on each other's growth, and both have found support in certain values implied in the

American dream. Managerial enterprise has gradually shifted emphasis from immediate profits to planning and a community of interests within the organization. Translated to the political sphere, these aims are the rationale for the welfare state. Both developments have increasingly illustrated the characeristics of bureaucracy, both have benefited from the American type of conformity and reliability, and both have operated on the basis of unique promise in American life. Both will require extended examination.

The evolution of the present welfare state is the background for the new developments in business leadership. Though denied over long periods in political pronouncements, the idea of government as a welfare device has always been present in the American states. In the early twentieth century, the powerful bipartisan Progressive movement openly adopted the welfare philosophy. While this wave of reform passed its flood tide in 1914 and reached a low ebb in national politics of the twenties, the flow of welfare legislation continued in the separate states. In many states the twenties were a decade of important implementation and improvement of the measures passed before the war.

But in the half-century before 1929 welfare activity had been associated with the poor or exploited, not with aid to business. It was the appalling rate of business recession in late 1931 that brought a dramatic change in the concept of legislation for the general welfare. Men of " the business world," wrote President Hoover, " threw up their hands and asked for government action." [5] With little regard to party lines a Democratic House, a Republican President, and a divided Senate agreed that a number of big businesses needed government support in order to survive. This was a different kind of welfare from early state subsidies to aid new business development or from the state's protection and care for weak and underprivileged individuals. This was the implicit assumption of an obligation to stabilize the economy.

Emergency action for business welfare, particularly the creation of the Reconstruction Finance Corporation, was a reluctant admission by believers in free enterprise that the business structure had become such a maze of financial interrelationships that it could no longer tolerate the impact of a major depression. It seems safe to assume that in America this marked an historical turning point. In the period before 1837 government had helped weak business; after 1850 strong business leaders had desired a weak state; now the two institutions were forced to enter into a precarious partnership with undefined obligations, but one from which neither could escape.

The partnership did not confine itself to aiding corporations by loans or stock subscriptions. The relentless downswing of the depression forced the federal government to assume the burdens of unemployment relief and old-age pensions, to underwrite home ownership and new housing, to subsidize agriculture, to interfere, that is, with the competitive struggle for survival of the fittest. With money taken in taxes the government had to do what individuals had hitherto been supposed to do for themselves. In arranging these matters neither partner trusted the other. Business favored most of the legislation designed to stimulate recovery but protested violently against laws designed to safeguard the public from bad business practices or to give labor more power. Government spokesmen, on their side, denounced business leaders as economic royalists and accused them of callousness and greed.

The law of supply and demand, so frequently invoked as a law of nature in business conversation, had long since been thwarted by open price policy and price leadership as well as by secret agreements. Nevertheless, the official suspension of the law of the market by the law of the land as expressed in the National Industrial Recovery Act symbolized a change of great significance. It meant that business would ultimately have to recognize that its classic creed or rationale was founded on doctrine that would no longer be adhered to by the government, that the whole theoretical economic structure built since Adam Smith's time must be revised with a view to adjusting it to what would really happen in situations where the economy was not self-regulating, where the state was prepared to take economic action.

While business leaders were groping toward a philosophy that would fit the apparent realities, British economist John Maynard Keynes came forward as an effective reviser of the classic doctrines. Keynes escaped the dilemma of the nature of relations between buyer and seller in the market by insisting that the more important relation was that between spender and investor. National income could go up, according to Keynes, only if investment increased, and increase in investment depended on business sentiment. That is, no matter how much might be saved, entrepreneurs would invest only where they judged they could recover their money with profit. Since the material welfare of society hinged upon increasing income, the matter was too important to be left dependent on business sentiment; government therefore was justified in stimulating and controlling investment.

Few heads of national states were Keynesian scholars, and the full formulation of his theory came late in the world-wide depression, but most political leaders acted pragmatically on Keynesian principles. Throughout the industrialized world, governments invested in roads, bridges, and buildings in an effort to prime the pump that would draw up capital for investment. In those countries that confined government investment to the area of traditional public works, the degree of recovery varied; in Great Britain it was fairly satisfactory, in the United States much less so. In Germany, where the government entered into basic industry for military purposes, a boom developed. It was the effects of massive government expenditures in World War II, however, rather than the feeble efforts of the depression period that drove the Keynesian lesson home to American politicians.

The profound discontent of business with the New Deal brand of salvation, and the failure of business leaders to win back the confidence of the public before 1940, contrast with the attitudes which World War II measures evoked. Many business leaders actively opposed war, but once a war of great magnitude and long duration became inevitable, the business-government partnership ceased being a reluctant one and began to operate with enthusiasm. Government spending for war production did not threaten to curtail the commercial market, did not appear to establish peace-time precedents, and was not designed to help people who should help themselves. " I think everyone who had to do with our aircraft work," wrote Chairman Paul Litchfield of Goodyear, " came out of the war with a deep feeling of satisfaction over it. Everyone wants to help his country in time of crisis." [6]

Relations between business and government were made pleasanter by the drafting of top executives like William Knudsen of General Motors and Donald Nelson of Sears,

Roebuck for federal administrative posts. A conversation with President K. T. Keller of Chrysler reported by Knudsen illustrates the new atmosphere. Knudsen wanted Keller to make tanks. Within a week Keller phoned:

" We can make them."

" How much will they cost? "

" Damned if I know—maybe $20,000 maybe $30,000. They weigh about thirty tons apiece."

" Yes, I know."

" I don't know what they will cost but that's my best guess now."

" I don't know either," replied Knudsen, " but figure it out as best you can—or, maybe we can work it out on a cost plus basis."

" I don't care how it's worked out," said Keller, " when do you want us to get going. . . ? "

At the end Knudsen added: " Send me a little piece of paper showing me what you spend—we've got to make it formal K. T." [7]

The return of peace was looked upon with apprehension by businessmen, economists, and workers. Many thought the dilemmas of 1939 would present themselves again. But they reckoned without the enormous pent-up demand of four years of saving from high incomes, four years without being able to buy the most popular or necessary kinds of durable goods. And just when the post-war boom had about run its course, the Korean War and higher levels of national defense touched off new private buying and government contracting.

Eighteen years have now passed without a serious recession, a record in American industrial history. Aided by their creditable performance in the war, business leaders have returned to popular favor, perhaps to the greatest popularity they have ever enjoyed. But comparisons are difficult. In the twenties business was the focus of American pride in material achievement. By the fifties, business was comfortably taken for granted and Americans were troubled about their achievements in other spheres.

The second of the two epoch-making changes to which I referred above is the development of managerial enterprise as a new and yet pervasive institutional form.

To many native Americans and to practically all foreigners, managerial enterprise, imperfectly understood, represents American business. In 1950, as in 1900, our people thought of business as dominated by the leaders of the big companies. If managerial enterprise has come to represent the most dynamic group of leaders in the business community, we must see how its values and trends fit in with the American dream. How does the professional manager fit into American society? This is a question difficult to answer.

The elements that have led to the development of mangerial enterprise are: widely held stock, directors who own a relatively small share in the company, and professional career executives who virtually control operations and dominate the board of directors but generally have only a small share in ownership. Beneath the top level are one or more layers of middle managers, each of whom hopes to rise in the executive pyramid.

Large banks and railroads have long illustrated this so-called " modern " type of corporation, but during the nineteenth century the operating managers were usually under the control of a few important capitalists. Men like Nathan Appleton, the Vanderbilts, the Rockefellers, or groups of lesser financiers dominated the boards on which they sat. Toward the end of the century, as companies grew bigger and stock became more widely held, representatives of the big investment banking houses assumed the mantles of the retiring pioneer capitalists. The ultimate wielder of power in New York Central, for example, came to be not one of the Vanderbilts but J. P. Morgan and Company. At about the same period General Motors was for five years controlled by a banking syndicate. It was this situation that prompted the " Money Trust " investigation by the House of Representatives in 1912, and led some scholars to say that " finance capitalism " had superseded industrial capitalism.

With investment bankers substituted for old-time financiers the shift to managerial enterprise was only partially complete. Since the bankers also worked with other people's money they could be regarded as managers, but they were managers controlling the board of directors from outside the family circle of the firm. The movement toward the pure form of inside control by officers alone for the benefit of the organization as such progressed rapidly during the twenties and thirties, as, first, an easy money market and, then, government regulations weakened the influence of the big financial houses.

The final triumph and public acceptance of managerial control by the fifties can be seen in the writing of scores of business commentators, as in the following recent example. In February, 1958, the Business Editor of *Time* wrote: " The Justice Department ordering partial breakup of the United Fruit Company sees no danger of interlocking control in a stock distribution to United stockholders. Officers of United hold less than .005% of the outstanding common, and 80% of the stockholders own less than 100 shares." [8] One is about to pass on to the next item of lucid opinion when suddenly the thought strikes—there was no mention of directors. They are skipped over because they no longer stand as the respected watchdogs of absent stockholders; they are merely the hired men with different hats on.

Since the 1920's, professional managers have become a generally recognized group with widely discussed social characteristics. Whereas the commentators of 1900 feared denial of opportunity by a few monopolists, those of the 1950's fear that the individualistic enterprising American of the classic dream will be replaced by the bureaucratic "organization man." This later fear is more basic. The earlier apprehension applied to an alteration in economic controls, while the modern anxiety applies to a fundamental change in national character and to the substitution of a conforming team-man for the thinking individual.

In trying to estimate the outlines of this problem, let us start with the social characteristics of the top managers. W. Lloyd Warner and James C. Abegglen have analyzed the careers of eighteen thousand top executives in large and medium-sized companies as of 1952.[9] The average executive had been to college—less than a quarter of these business leaders lacked some college training. The leader's father had usually been a business owner or executive or a professional man born in the United States, and his paternal grandfather had the same occupational characteristics, if one includes running or managing a farm with hired help as an executive position. The average leader was city-bred from a place of over twenty-five thousand inhabitants; he married a girl whose father was a business or professional man.

In spite of this picture of an upper-middle class, or socially elite background for men at the top, occupational mobility was increasing in American big business. Careful comparison with a similar study by Taussig and Joselyn in 1928 shows that in the former year only sixteen per cent of the business leaders had fathers who were laborers or white-collar workers, whereas in the later group twenty-three per cent of the leaders had such paternity.[10] Further analysis also shows that upward mobility was greater in large corporations than in small, so that some of our assumed increase in " economic democracy " may have arisen from the growth of American corporations in size and impersonality.

In the office these educated careerists are expected to play a different social role from that of the profit-seeking smaller businessman. In many ways the latter can be a rough diamond; he can rant and curse and be personally obnoxious as long as he produces his goods or services efficiently. He can be selfish, grasping, and myopic regarding his relations to society as long as he deals satisfactorily with his customers. The career executive trying to rise in a large company can afford few of these weaknesses. First and foremost he has to be a team-man, an organization man. " Let me remind you," said William Stephen of Goodyear, " that we can't consider anyone for promotion unless he has built a smooth-running organization." [11] A manager must be liked by his superiors, must be pleasant to associate with in endless conferences and meetings. In some companies the manager must pass personality tests. His commitment must be to the welfare of the firm, conceived broadly. Loyalty and teamwork are essential, while an innovating intelligence is something extra that may or may not be wanted.

Much of this interpretation of the executive's role in big companies is not new. Some of its elements had been perceived in the early days. In 1885 Charles E. Perkins, president of the Chicago, Burlington and Quincy Railroad, wrote: " Every man is entitled to his own private opinions, but every man who works for a railroad company is nevertheless bound to carry out its policy in matters where it has policy, and to do this in good faith regardless of private opinions." [12] The aim of loyalty and teamwork is, of course, a steady and dependable profit for the corporation, but this goal can be pursued not so much by penny-pinching efficiency or smart market operations as by cultivating good relations with all interested parties.

The professional manager, no longer expecting to get rich by a lucky stroke, and usually well taken care of from the standpoint of salary, looks to other sources than wealth for satisfaction or marks of success. Gratifying the expectations of his fellow executives is one of the most immediate sources of satisfaction. Thus, social roles tend to become more sharply defined, conduct becomes more conventional, and the importance of personal relations is magnified. David Riesman and his associates have called this an " overpersonalized society." [13]

In other ways leadership in the managerial system operates differently from the age-old system of owner-management. The new doctrine leads to a different division of gains, for those with face-to-face contacts will tend to get more than absentees. Higher salaries and wages are likely to take precedence over dividends to unknown stockholders. Large financial reserves are accumulated to insure the life of the growing concern, whether or not this accords with maximum short-run economic gain for the absentee owners.

69

These are the fundamental relationships of managerial enterprise and it is at once obvious that they are inevitably altering the character of capitalism. Once the major aim is transferred from profit for stockholders to the welfare of the organization as such, the critical step has been taken in the direction of a new social system. Planning comes to be in terms of how the organization can best adjust to general social trends so as to insure survival over many years, how it can continually raise the compensation of its employees to sustain loyalty and morale. As Professor Drucker put it: " It is management's public responsibility to *make* whatever is genuinely in the public good *become* the enterprise's own self-interest." [14] There are still few managements that have reached this conscious degree of enlightenment. In fact, the leaders of many big companies would deny that any such change has taken place. Furthermore, even if the manager is no longer a ruthless profit seeker, he may be ruthless in seeking prestige and personal fame. But there is a difference in that, while profit may accrue from private vice, social prestige has to come from what must at least appear to be public virtue.

The appropriateness of maintaining that the growth of the big private corporation and the rise of the welfare state are essentially the same in their effects on cultural change should now be clear. Both emphasize long-run security rather than adventurous risk-taking; both define success in terms of a democratic careerism within a bureaucratic organization; both reward the cooperative conforming personality. The following advice, given in the forties by a railroad president to a young boy, would apply equally well to a career in government or one in business: " Industry and cooperation are very important," he said; " teamwork is as essential on a railroad as it is on a football field. . . . Cultivate and develop a pleasing and friendly personality. . . . Show an interest in other people and what they have to say. . . . Finish college." [15]

The added value placed on conformity or normal responses in men who wish to succeed was well put by David Sarnoff, chairman of the Board of Radio Corporation of America: " On the basis of our experience the single most important factor determining whether a man is a really satisfactory employee . . . is . . . his family life. If he has a normal, happy family life with a good home he is a satisfied normal fellow. If he hasn't got it—if he has a nag for a wife, for example, . . . he isn't going to be worth a damn because he isn't normal and he isn't going to be able to keep his mind on his daily work." [16] A Commodore Vanderbilt, with his unhappy married life and his irascible disposition, would not have been a promising junior executive.

In some advanced management thinking of the fifties the corporation is seen as a community. " We live Woolworth," said President James F. Leftwich.[17] According to Herrymon Maurer: " The chief executives of many companies have stressed group-mindedness so emphatically as a motive fundamental to the management of any large corporate body, and executives have been motivated so strongly that the managers of some corporations have developed group traits and characteristics different from those of other executive bodies." [18] Frank Abrams, president of Standard Oil of New Jersey, also seems to regard the corporation as a kind of welfare community: " Modern management might well measure its success or failure as a profession in large part by the satisfactions it is able to produce for its employees." [19]

Obviously such an organizational welfare approach

may develop economic weaknesses, but the big company selling at administered prices can afford these. Managerial employees may be raised in rank and salary to maintain morale or " satisfaction " when their productivity does not justify it or be retained because of tenure understandings when their jobs are no longer necessary. The lowered ratio of employees to production in some big companies in the depressions of 1920-22 and 1930-34 suggests how much flexibility there has been in size of staff. Furthermore, expenditures which will improve or add prestige to the organization as such, although the effect on profit is not clear, may be preferred to the payment of larger dividends to stockholders, to the realization, that is, of profit by the owners.

The influence of big business leaders on other companies and on society in general has beyond question grown concurrently with increased management control inside business. The growing prestige of big business is a trend which has been " viewed with alarm " and sometimes discussed with heat. The facts neither completely prove nor totally deny an increase in influence that would justify alarm.

It is in manufacturing that big companies have had their greatest influence on smaller ones. Apparently independent smaller companies are occasionally subcontractors or exclusive suppliers for larger ones. But the power relationships here are complex. The big company needs the smaller ones and cannot afford a bad reputation in its relations with them. The owner-managers of the small companies are generally free to make all the profit they can from increased efficiency or additional activities. More important still, if one checks the various manufacturing enterprises in a medium-sized city, there may be only a few that are dependent in any important way on continuous contracts with one or two big companies.

While rail and public utility companies are usually big business, they are so strictly regulated that they have little opportunity to wield coercive influence. Their leaders are generally not free to expand company operations into new fields or to pursue policies that may lead to domination over other business.

In retail and wholesale trade and in service—the major areas of American and of world-wide business activity— the growth of big enterprise has been slow. Retailers in some lines were forced in the thirties to get together in voluntary chains supplied by common wholesalers, but after this the spread of corporate chains was arrested. The picture remained one of competitive local business, whose prices were not effectively controlled by big suppliers.

Political and social influence in all but a few cities appears to be in the hands of the leading *local* businessmen: the successful manufacturers, brokers, undertakers, lawyers, wholesalers, and retailers. If their decisions in civic matters have been guided by the wishes of the leaders of the giant corporations it is not apparent to interviewers. Some sizable cities may have no important representatives of any big national companies.

The case for the influence of the executives of big companies has to rest more on political pressures at state or national levels and on sophisticated leadership in business and social affairs. The first type of influence is necessarily hard to estimate. It is secret, and highly personal. Its trail is only uncovered by occasional investigations. Amid the competition of lobbyists for every kind of public and private interest, those representing big business, to be sure, usually have more money to work with and better contacts with high government officials. But this influence has probably been more effective in the states when state governments were in a position to act than it has in the federal government.

From the standpoint of effects on managerial and social practice, the case for the influence of the big businessman is strong. The big company has specialists studying its problems. The findings of these men are read in business magazines and trade journals and applied by smaller companies. The public relations departments of large firms supply a disproportionate number of speakers to public occasions, men whose prestige comes from their position in the big company. Management, engineering, accounting, and other consultants make reputations by being called upon by big companies. In some cases the use of consulting firms by smaller companies is probably just a matter of keeping up with the Joneses.

In general the real situation is much harder to define than the arbitrary models set up by some economists and journalists suggest. If the leaders of big corporations were to cooperate closely in a political or social campaign they could exert tremendous pressure. But the tendency seems to have been not to cross industry lines except on a few general political issues. There does not appear to have been any closely knit "power elite." If such cooperative action by a single group were attempted, the leaders would run the risk of reprisals by other groups such as farmers, labor, or small business. There is truth in J. K. Galbraith's idea of countervailing powers. In a similar vein, Peter K. Drucker warns: " I recommend that management religiously avoid asserting or assuming responsibility for any activities it does not want to see controlled by the union leaders or by government." [20]

From the twenties on, the leaders of the biggest companies gradually became conscious of the complex interests of the corporation in a democratic society. Public relations policies were overhauled. Favorable news releases and good-will advertising proved inadequate in the depression of the thirties. Something more substantial was required.

The big company needed to prove that it was a good citizen of the many communities in which it had plants and offices. The new policy was pursued slowly and cautiously. Spending the stockholder's money for community welfare projects was opposed to the classic doctrines of trusteeship. Many would still have agreed with railroad president John W. Brooks who said in 1871: " Our mission is not that of aiding institutions for religion or learning because they commend themselves to our personal judgment. . . . We can properly help . . . when it is clearly for the pecuniary advantage of our stockholders that we should do so. . . ." [21] It could be argued that this view never changed, but the " pecuniary advantage " of the stockholders was, by the late forties, being very broadly interpreted, and this interpretation was supported in the courts.

Branches were supplied with public relations men, and branch managers were given funds for contributions to local civic campaigns. In the Du Pont precinct system, for example, each plant manager became responsible for good public relations in his area. This meant that he was expected to assume civic leadership and responsibility. To a considerable degree big companies have become reconciled to bowing to public opinion. The great prosperity from 1940 to 1957 made good relations easier. The big companies have paid the highest wages and have been able to offer the most security and fringe benefits.

Stockholders who had once been thought of primarily as a troublesome group likely to interfere with management came to be regarded as a public relations resource. A hundred thousand stockholders were seen as that many citizens with a personal interest in the welfare of the company. Campaigns were put on to distribute stock more widely, shares were subdivided if their price rose too high for the small investor, and company reports took on a public relations look.

To satisfy the American desire to have all positions of power based on reason and utility, the public relations men of big business developed the theory of consumer sovereignty or democracy. Companies, they argued, grow big by satisfying the customer. Management retains authority only by the same sanction. The consumer's purchases are votes which he, or more often she, casts in favor of this corporation or that. Advertising is the indispensable medium by which the consumer voter is kept informed of what is on the ballot. No matter how big a company may become, its wares have to be popular or the company leaders will not survive.

The argument, however, is true only within certain limits. There has to be some real choice open to the buyer. If the articles in question are of standard design and equal price, produced by two or three companies that have well worked-out agreements, the consumer's desires may be of secondary importance; what competition exists is for outlets; the customer buys the brand the dealer sells. The same negation of consumer democracy exists in the case of most public utilities and of products protected by patents. Furthermore, the pressure of consumer democracy on a weak management works slowly. It might require ten years of relative decline in sales to bring action by some powerful financial group to overthrow the existing regime. But perhaps lack of immediate power is inherent in all indirect democracy.

The great corporation, with its especially created career leadership, with shifting motivation and values, and with community and public responsibility, is an institution of a new type of capitalism. The new leadership is having to find its place in an American culture whose values are also changing.

Though Americans at the turn of the century worried about monopolists, the values professed by these business leaders were generally accepted. From the downfall of the planters as champions of an aristocratic agrarian sub-culture to the Great Depression, a businesslike approach to life was not seriously challenged. The distinction between intellectuals and men of action was strictly observed to the disadvantage of the former. No group of intellectuals, as such, was looked to for national leadership. The prestige of the academic profession was diluted by an extreme localism in higher education that produced thousands of poorly paid professors of uncertain ability and indifferent learning. A branch of the Protestant ministry did combat business values, but the richest and most influential parishes kept becoming more and more businesslike. " How cautious is the church—as an organiza-tion—in taking a stand that might lift the bristles of a financial interest," wrote the well known sociologist E. A. Ross.[22] Some farmers have always attacked business, but their attacks have been in terms of such business considera-tions as higher prices and lower costs, and, in any case, they have scarcely influenced the urban groups that have perpetuated and shaped national culture.

As late as the fifties, in the mass-circulation newspapers and magazines, on radio and television, what was good for business was accepted as good for the nation. Any proposal that was unbusinesslike or endangered business prosperity had little chance of a full presentation in these media. But beneath the surface, business thinking at mid-century is far more troubled than it was in 1900. The managerial ideology so emphasizes education, cooperation, and success through personal relations and disapproves so strongly of egotistic individualism, ruthless dealings with competitors, and any quest for high profits dangerous to long-run security, that the managerial creed of the fifties seems to be in a transition stage away from the classic ideas toward a rationale for a basically political rather than an acquisitive culture—toward a doctrine in which the goal is to achieve a position that confers power and prestige rather than personal wealth.

But the classic business aim of gaining individual wealth from competition is still pursued by the millions of small enterprisers, even though their views are much less reflected in advertising, journalism, literature or art than are the views of the managerial leaders. This internal conflict in attitudes makes it hard to speak of the business ideology of the mid-twentieth century. Alhough William Whyte in his well-known *Organization Man* may somewhat exaggerate, there seems little doubt that in the conflict of values the managerial attitude, the team-man view, is becoming stronger and more widespread. Business leaders are moving by force of circumstance from emphasis on individual innovation and brilliance toward sponsorship of divided responsibility, team-work, and bureaucratic devices.

The partnership between business and government to maintain American world leadership, to carry out the American mission, works strongly in favor of the attitudes of the advanced managerial leaders. The critical importance of defense and foreign-aid contracts to much of big business has put executives in politics as never before. Companies have hired retiring generals and admirals for their Washington contacts, thereby creating a new military-political segment of corporate leadership. These political and international relationships force executives to try to see their company activities from the outside, to see more clearly how they affect public opinion and what part they are playing in foreign relations.

While these close ties to government and the military seem to assure, through continued long-run prosperity, that businessmen will maintain their economic position in the emerging society, such ties involve challenges in values from powerful competing forces in the culture. Value systems stemming from religion, the paternalistic state, and the heroic as represented by the military have always been the three complexes that could conceivably supersede the values of business. The New Deal and World War II gave the national state and the armed forces stronger positions in American culture. While the military is a part of the paternalistic state, from the standpoint of certain values the two institutions are opposed. The military stands for leadership, discipline, courage, and sacrifice for national honor. The political state stands for democracy, compromise, and security. Will the new goals or ultimate values of corporate leadership be influenced most by those of social democracy or by the military or

79

even by some new form of religion? Will they perpetuate the American dream of equal opportunity, a free society, and individualism?

Those leaders of business who are seeking to preserve the classic creed like to think of themselves as being closer to the military virtues, although in fact they are probably moving ever closer to those of the welfare state. But a major barrier to the ultimate acceptance of the value system of the welfare state by those business leaders who profess the new managerial creed is the practice of democracy. For nearly three hundred years, or until moderately big business became the employer of over a quarter of the working population, the contradiction between democracy in politics and authoritarianism in business had not seemed serious. But after World War II, when big businessmen were seen both at home and abroad as spokesmen for the American social system, the discrepancy began to appear serious. Mr. O. P. Wheeler, a prominent Westcoast banker, warned: " This inability to achieve a democratic system of operation on a widespread scale within the company or firm, the failure to develop participative policy formation to any marked degree, and the unwillingness or inability to consider seriously and to respond to the problems and values of American society indicate characteristics quite at variance with the main stream of American social life or culture." [23]

Forces within the ranks of managerial leadership, however, are operating to lessen the conflict in values. Consultants in industrial relations have begun to advise democratic procedures as an aid to worker morale. Discussions in committees and conferences, sometimes with free interchange of ideas, lead lower-level employees to feel that they have a voice in policy formation. This is, to be sure, not democracy in the classic sense; management does not stand for election by fellow employees; policies are not subject to a legal referendum of those concerned; but explanation and discussion *are* a recognition of the importance of employee opinion.

In summary, a small group of professional managers has come to play a leading part in changing business attitudes and motives. Public approval, personal prestige, employee welfare and morale, and the security of the organization have risen as goals alongside the age-old quest for profits. Genial, conforming personality has been rewarded, and skillful playing of quasi-political roles demanded. But what have these changes meant for the operation of the economic system?

The relative maturity of mangerial enterprise is too recent for us to be sure of its over-all impact on the economy. The pressures seem to be those that arise from primary emphasis on the welfare of the organization. Because the organization benefits, wages tend to move up more readily than in earlier decades; prices, largely administered, tend to rise rather than fall; large reserves tend to take precedence over dividends; innovation tends to be relegated to specialized departments, while closely defined roles may tend to discourage innovation in general administration; less aggressive, more conforming entrepreneurs tend to rise to the top; and college graduates without money tend to have a better chance to get ahead than ever before. It seems impossible to separate the effects of these factors from those of others in the economy. To what extent, for example, is inflation caused by managerial enterprise and to what extent is it caused by capital investment that has been exceeding savings? One can only suggest that economists take more account of these qualitative changes in the entrepreneurial situation.

The sheltered areas of large-scale managerial enterprise, in which welfare flourishes, are always menaced by destructive gales of competition that threaten to carry customers away to new products. There are six million small businessmen in America who have not risen through organizations, who run their own shops, and who are avid for profit. There seems little immediate prospect of reconciliation between the single-minded creed of these small businessmen and the complex philosophy of the managers of big enterprise. But since the latter ideology is more publicized, conforms better to the non-business values of the American heritage, suits the aims of the welfare state, and better justifies American world leadership, it has an outer strength denied to earlier business creeds. Whether it has the inner strength to endure a prolonged downswing in profits remains to be seen.

IV

The Dream in the Urban Age

American Civilization in the Post-Rural Day

MAX LERNER

Professor of American Civilization
Brandeis University

The Dream in the Urban Age

I CHOOSE to use both the word "civilization" and the word "culture" almost interchangeably—I say "almost" because I note that the term "civilization" disturbed some reviewers of my book, *America as a Civilization*. Some of our British reviewers especially have wondered how you can use the word "America" and the word "civilization" in juxtaposition. It is as if they were looking at us and saying: "This crude, raw, unfinished, barbaric collection of shards and fragments of peoples from every part of the world, of the traditions and habits of thought they have brought with them, of the new attitudes that have emerged—do you call this a *civilization?*"

But I use "civilization" because I want to convey a certain meaning with it. When a people has evolved characteristic ways of thinking and behaving that make it different from other peoples in history—different, for example, from Rome, and Greece, and Russia, and India, and China—and when it has cut a wide swath in history and left an impact for good or ill upon the consciousness of the world, then you have something that is worth calling a civilization. This doesn't mean that it is necessarily superior to others or necessarily original. Nor does it mean that there is a kind of grocery or laundry list of what we call "national traits" that this people possesses. But it does mean that there are certain characteristic internal patterns it posesses, forming a "figure in the carpet," as Henry James put it.

I suggest that we set this cultural "figure in the carpet" side by side with several of the historical dream images of American culture, such as the Jeffersonians or Jacksonians had, or the social reformers at the turn of the twentieth century. When you do so, the contrast is sharp. The model of America that we have inherited, and that many still carry around in their minds, is the model of a relatively simple society of sturdy yeomen, farmers, and workers, very much like the citizenry of the Greek city-state. It is a model of standards set from above by a group of cultivated people and borrowed colonially from Europe. It is a model of the locality as the unit of work, leisure, and play—of local schools, local press, local workshops, local leisure, all of them locally controlled.

This is the picture. And obviously, like most idyllic pictures, it doesn't work. What we have seen in the past half-century, since the Progressive Era, has been a series of revoltions. I use the term "revolution," not in the narrower technical sense of a shift in class power, but as a drastic and radical transformation in any area of life. In that sense we have had a succession of revolutions in recent American history. We have had the continuing revolution of the machine, which made a foreign architect and planner, Siegfried Gideon, note that "mechanization takes command" in America; with mechanization has come the phenomenon of large-scale investment needed to carry on mechanized enterprise. We have had, second, the emergence of the big opinion industries in America— the big media, including the press and all the other media which shape opinion. We have had, third, the emergence of the city that Professor Miller mentions—the city and its streets—and more recently the suburb as well. We have had, fourth, the creation of a vast democratic mass, highly pluralistic, coming from the twelve corners of the earth, bringing different cultures, traditions, languages, even religions. We have had, fifth, the task of the education of this democratic mass. Last, we have the emergence of a " mass culture " or " popular culture," which we call by those names to distinguish it from " elite " culture or " high " culture.

Thus the dream on the one hand, the reality on the other. Instead of treating the two as separated by a gap, I prefer to say that the reality that lies around us is the material with which all of us have to work as artists, since a democracy requires civic artists. We cannot look back nostalgically to a less complex era nor hope that the reality will be simpler than the truth. We have to use this material and make out of it something close to our dream, rethinking the dream in the light of what we have at our command and the tasks ahead of us. This makes of it what one might call a contemporary dream.

The writer who saw this problem most clearly was Walt Whitman, who wrote of it in his *Democratic Vistas.* He saw sharply the chaos of political and moral corruption that had already set in. He knew something about the mass of the people, yet did not have snobbish and ironic contempt for them but accepted them with affection. He foresaw that they would have to acquire leadership to develop a great culture and gave a very special name to the leader—the " divine literatus." He saw this leader as a man of letters and of thought, who was " divine " only in the sense that he had some feeling about the essential dignity of the ordinary person and about the relationship between the cultural potential and the high cultural standards that every culture sets for itself. I sometimes wonder what Walt Whitman would make of our democratic scene in the mid-1950's and what democratic vistas he would see. Very humbly I want to speak in his spirit, with the same affection and respect for the basic human material in our country, without the ironic contempt which highbrow intellectuals are expected to feel toward the mass of people and the popular culture, but also with exacting standards of thought, taste, and creativeness, and with a jealous zeal for the greatness of our country and culture.

This America of ours is changing almost underneath our fingers. I had a curious experience with my own book, if I may speak of that. It was twelve years in the writing. During those twelve years, as I went through successive drafts, I found that the civilization sitting for the portrait wouldn't sit still but kept moving and being transformed all the time. If we look back to the America of the Progressive Era and look at the America of today, the changes are even more drastic.

For example, I started with the city, but at the end the city was no longer the growing point: that was now the new suburbia and the new exurbia—all the ways we have of crowding together in order to find living space. When I started, the industrial revolution had not reached the phase of automation which is in full swing today— revolution which can liberate the mass of people from repetitive and dreary tasks and give men a new kind of job, not the job of running the machines, which machines themselves are now doing, but the job of seeing to it that the machines which run machines won't break down. Along with this liberation from work routine I found a do-it-yourself movement by which Americans were seeking a new sense of a piece of work as an organic whole in its relation to themselves as human beings. I found an America which had discovered in nuclear energy new ways of killing people and new ways of dying, but also a medical revolution which had discovered new ways of saving people's lives and new ways of living longer. I found the new phenomenon of the public relations counsel with new ways of persuasion. I found an America in which the phrase " motivational research " had come into being, along with the phrase " subliminal persuasion " for the ways of reaching people below the threshold of their consciousness. It was also an America with an expense-account aristocracy which kept a lot of hotels and restaurants and airlines from bankruptcy.

It was the America of a new cooking revolution, which had found new ways of whipping up something unique and individual out of cans. It was the America of liberated women who, once they had found their freedom, were not quite sure what they wanted to do with it; of liberated women, moreover, who, with all their leisure, carried a greater burden of duties than perhaps any other population of women in the past. I found an America of Kinsey surveys, which proved to be the greatest organized manifestation in history of the urge to confide. I found an America that was hacking new roads through the jungle of psychiatry. I found an America with the burden of new leisure which it was not prepared to meet. It was an America with a new baby-boom and a monster rally of young people storming the gates of the colleges. It was an America with changing dating patterns. When I started my book I had a section on " dating-rating " patterns, which showed young people dating someone different every night. But when I tried this on my students at Brandeis, they told me this was archaic and what they had now was

89

steady dating. So I had to get acquainted with steady dating—that precocious, dreary fidelity of two young people toward each other, not out of conviction but out of poverty of imagination.

I found an America of the servantless family. But the America of the absentee husband and father, which was a fact when I started, had been changed; the husband had come back into the family and the home; in fact, he came back into the kitchen, where they put an apron around him and set him to work. I found also an America of the paperback revolution. I found an America that was using stimulants to pep you up and tranquilizers to quiet you down.

This was our America. And yet, impressionistic though the picture may be, I think, it is suggestive both of the pace of change and of the refusal to follow patterns imposed by any group of moralists or moralizers; suggestive also because it conveys the outlines of a popular culture.

I should like first to speak generally about popular culture as a whole. There has never been anything quite like this task that America is undertaking, that of hewing out a new way of life, taking the city and its new suburbs and satellites and introducing some tolerable living conditions within all of this congestion and frantic haste. It is also the task of trying to fit into a frame of order the living standards and leisure that the machine has made possible. Nothing on such a scale has ever been attempted in history, within a structure of political freedom and relatively free inquiry and with indirect rather than direct controls.

I put it in these terms because the Russians, and more recently the Chinese, have also tried to fashion a new culture, and they have done it in some ways on a larger scale than ours. They too have had some of the difficulties of trying to pull together diverse ethnic groups, but they have proceeded under the principle of total control—the principle set by a group that somehow knew what was right and what was to be followed by the peoples. I am not now going to prejudge how those cultural experiments will come out, but I do suggest that the fact that the Russians and the Chinese have undertaken so vast an experiment does not diminish the uniqueness of our task, because it comes within this frame of individual freedom and relatively free inquiry and with the use of indirect and not direct controls.

Of course, we have to say that we have not succeeded wholly, but the fact that we have any success at all is the true miracle, considering the immensity of the problem. Let us remember that the standards of an aristocratic society, a society of tight status, one of stratified norms of conduct, one of elite arts, do not apply to us. We are a mobile, fluid, open society with constantly shifting stratification, with no hereditary aristocracy to lay down norms of conduct or taste, and not even with any great traditions of high culture to carry on. We started from a wilderness, and although we inherited much of the elite culture of Europe we also rejected it to a very great extent. All through American history there has been the preference for what is indigenously American as against the elite culture of Europe.

In a true sense, we have been culturally revolutionary. We have given scope, for example, in our movies to the energies of a Chaplin, or a Garbo, or a Griffith, or a Disney; in the press we have given scope to the energies of a Pulitzer or a Scripps or a Heywood Broun; on the musical comedy stage we have given scope to the energies of an Agnes De Mille, or a Hammerstein and Rogers, or a Cole Porter. We have taken serious writers and composers and artists and given them access to an audience such as no group of elite artists and writers has ever had before. It was W. H. Auden who remarked that the great revolution of our time lies in the fact that we can now make the whole cultural heritage of the world available to all the people at any time; if we release the creative imagination and if we can get the people to open their minds to it, this increased dissemination of the heritage of culture can be achieved. As regards the fine arts, André Malraux spoke of a "museum without walls" in modern times, a phrase which can be applied not only to painting but to the whole of culture. This development has required the creation of new methods, new media, new technological forms, new forms of business organization, new forms of governmental control.

In bringing about our cultural revolution we have not imitated Europe or classical antiquity and, therefore, should not be judged solely by their standards. Instead, the criteria of judgment should be in terms of the nature of the experiments we have undertaken. But our indigenous forms are now influencing Europe. A talented newspaperman, Blair Bolles, has written a book called *The Big Change in Europe* in which he points out that anyone who studies Western Europe today sees in it new technological changes, changes in the former proletariat of Europe, changes in the big media, changes in popular culture which can only be ascribed to the revolutionary impact of America. The process, thus, has been a dual one. We derived much from what we carried from Europe, and now Europe, in turn, is beginning to feel the effect of what we have developed. These cultural exports of ours are not necessarily good; some of them are very poor, and some even vicious. The kind of movies that we send around the world should never have been exported; in fact, they should perhaps never been made. The emphasis on salesmanship, the emphasis on the deployment of the human being as an object for the manipulative energies of the deployer—these influences of America are not good. But the new situation is certainly not all bad either; it is revolutionary and is characterized by a two-way process between ourselves and the rest of the world.

What of the quality of what we have accomplished? Much of what might have been creative has been diluted and homogenized, to be cheaply vendable. We have often worshiped the false gods of the market place of success, and power and money. These values clearly need to be transformed.

But for the first time in history, within a free system, the whole of a people has taken part in the creation of a culture. When, for example, I seek about in my mind to find the most creative thing about American culture, the thing on which I fix is American speech. The American language is not the creation of a small group, but the creation of the whole mass. Labor gangs, construction workers, convicts working on the road, longshoremen, young people obsessed with music and dances—all of us have had some kind of hand in the shaping of this great artifact of America. All of us have given it a constantly new vitality so that it has become a thing that is rich, flexible, and full of resourcefulness. Another aspect of our culture which I regard as creative is jazz. American jazz as an idiom was brought over from West Africa, Latin America, the Caribbean, and Spain, and grew in the brothels and in the honky-tonks of New Orleans. It somehow was charged with the energy of a lusty people emerging from slavery into a dawning sense of the world's dimensions and possibilities. A people that had been starved for expression made jazz, not just a music form, but an expression of the whole pace of American life. In speech and in jazz, in television and even occasionally in the movies, we have here a culture in the making with all of us as participants.

Fun is made of the child-oriented anarchy that constitutes the American family. Fun is made of the absentee father, of the mother loaded down with too many burdens, of the cacophonous brats, of the Kinsey surveys, and of the Gesell books and Dr. Spock and all the rest. Yet, one may see the American family as perhaps the most exciting experiment in democracy that we have undertaken. We are, as a people, making an effort to take the primary form of social organization and to develop it, not as an authoritarian form, but as a means to freedom and equality in the whole emotional structure of family relationships— between husband and wife, between parents and children, between siblings themselves. We have been at it a short time, and to a great extent chaos still reigns, yet looking at the long-range trend I cannot doubt that we are moving toward greater order, cohesiveness, and effectiveness in family relations. The American woman, again for the first time in history, is learning both to develop herself as a person and at the same time to be part of the whole family constellation. She is having to pay a heavy price for it in conflict and unhappiness, just as many of us are having to pay a heavy price for daring to undertake these experiments in a democratic society. Yet when people write long books, drawing a parallel between America and

94

Rome and using the family as proof that we are sliding down the slope to destruction as Rome did, I can only say that it is not the picture I see.

As I look toward the American future I see certain agenda for greatness. One item in these agenda has to do with education, a second with opinion and freedom, a third with creativeness.

First, on education. There is a great debate going on now, much of it directed to the question of how we can best tap the talent that our young people have. I should like to suggest that the real intellectual resources of America are not being tapped, not so much because we are not teaching the right courses, as so many contemporary commentators seem to think, but because we still have so many roadblocks on the road to educational opportunity. I am speaking of the roadblocks of color, of religion, of the impoverished family, of the backward state with too low an educational budget. I am thinking of the young people who, because they are of the wrong color or religion or income group, do not get a chance to show their potential ability.

The important race in which we are engaged now is not a weapons race, it is an intelligence race. Some of the educational critics are having fun attacking the " life-adjustment " courses and the all too obvious illiteracy of some of our young people. But we must recognize that these are the product of a vaster effort at mass education than has perhaps ever been undertaken. It is time for us to move to another phase of our educational revolution. We have used education to promote cohesion among our ethnic groups and to give them some civic understanding. It is time that we began in earnest the effort to create what

Thomas Jefferson dreamt of, a democratic elite—an elite of talent based, not on heredity or on an aristocracy, but on the selective processes of a democracy. It is more important for our young to stretch themselves to the farthest limits of their potential capacity than to send another satellite into orbit or try to send a rocket to the moon. The problem of education is a problem of moving from mass education, although not abandoning it, to selective education, and, in doing so, confronting the problem of subsidizing talented young people whenever necessary. My definition of education is the heroic encounter between two people, a teacher and a student, each of whom, in the process, is stretching himself. What we need to do is to give our young people, as never before, this chance to stretch themselves.

The second item in the agenda for greatness has to do with another form of education, not the schools, but the media which shape the stereotypes in the minds of both our young people and our adults. A new elite of corporate managers has occupied strategic positions which give them access to the shaping of people's minds. Those strategic positions are in the press, in radio, in television, in all of the communication media. What we have been witnessing in the half-century since the Progressive Era in the press, for example, is a kind of cannibalism in which papers have eaten each other, so that there are fewer and fewer of them, and local communities have in most cases given up the effort at genuine competition of ideas. What we called the "one-party press," which is to me not a very happy phrase, represent a core of reality. It is not so much that it is a one-party press; the crucial element is that a true competition of ideas is narrowed. There has, as well, been a drying up of crusading spirit

96

on the part of the press—a natural consequence of the occupation of strategic positions by a small group.

But the thing that I find most dreary and frightening is the fear of controversy that has developed in the very medium where controversy is essential. There was, for example, a time when it was considered subversive to say a good word for a man named Professor Oppenheimer. Recently, by the way, one of our German missile experts, Dr. Von Braun, said something quite brave about Dr. Oppenheimer; he said that if this were England Oppenheimer would have been knighted. Actually, what we did with this man, instead of putting a garland around his head, was to give him hemlock to drink, as the Greeks did to Socrates. There was a time when we were afraid to say a word for him and it is this fear of the controversial which to me represent one of the greatest dangers that we face. There are, of course, some reasons for it. America is pluralistically constituted of many ethnic groups, religious groups, geographic regions, economic classes, and we fear to step on the toes of any of them; we are afraid that anyone speaking up will somehow hurt them. It is unfortunately true that we are also afraid of stepping on the toes of those who represent majority power and privilege. One of the difficult tasks of freedom in America is to develop a great dialogue—between leaders, between peoples, and among people in general. In order to develop the great dialogue you must have a competition of ideas and you must have the courage to insist that America cannot create a great culture *without* such a competition.

The third item in the agenda of American greatness has to do with creativeness. It is very difficult to maintain creativeness in the opinion industries and in the big media, whose essence is, of course, standardized reproduction. It is aways cheaper per unit to print six million books than six hundred thousand and cheaper to print six hundred thousand than six thousand. It is better to have a two-year run or a three-year run of a play on Broadway than a small one. It is better and easier to make money by selling a huge audience to a sponsor than by selling a small one. The very nature of the mechanical revolution seems to have brought with it an accommodation of thought to the mass, a process of homogenizing and of dilution. I see no necessity for it.

What has happened in our culture is that we have taken the dynamism of American life and we have given it expression in the external aspects of our culture, but we have failed to internalize the dynamic in our own thinking. There is a sense of geographical mobility and of social mobility in America, a cult of bigness and of speed, which the popular arts express. But we have allowed our thinking and our attitudes to become so rigid that inner growth has been stifled. In the gap between the rapid pace of the externals in American life and the inner rigidity we may find an indictment of our conformity. Obviously conformity exists and must exist, to some extent, in every society. But what we really mean when we speak of conformity in America is that we have taken the area of our selfhood, the area of individual identity, and have allowed it to become tyrannized.

There are certain things that need to be done in the reconstruction or liberation of the American personality in the calculable future. One of the most important is the quest for identity, the daring to be yourself, the daring to mock and to reject the gods of the culture—the gods of success and power and money and prestige and security. We must be willing to look at ourselves in the mirror of ourselves rather than in the mirror of others. We must make the journey into the interior; we must turn inward, dream, have idle thoughts, non-utilitarian and unprofitable thoughts that will never make us rich or famous. We must rediscover the world of sensibility, the capacity to feel nature—the carpet of the earth and the tent of the sky. And finally we must reaffirm a sense of human connection, the nexus of individuals with other individuals.

What I am suggesting now when I speak of this reconstruction of the American personality goes much further than a mere stand against conformity. I am speaking rather of what Lewis Mumford has called the "transformations of man." Mankind has already passed through a number of transformations, and if we are to survive the contemporary crisis another great transformation must take place now.

I end with some words on rigidity. When I came to the end of my book, I tried to sum up what seemed to me the crucial single thing I felt about America as I looked ahead. The feeling I had was that the great enemy is not the Russians, nor the subversives within, but rigidity— the rigidifying of the mind, the incapacity to meet new situations with new ideas and new strategies.

One may find among the Greeks and in other cultures the legend of the "heroic encounter"—the hero who slays the lion (or bull or dragon) and puts the lion's skin over his shoulder. But actually the heroic encounter is not between the hero and the lion; it is inside the hero, inside the human being. The real battle is between the forces of creativeness and destructiveness, of resiliency and rigidity within us and within our whole social system and culture.

If anyone says to me, "You speak with some affirmation

about American culture, but how about the dark and seamy sides of the American experience—how about the anti-Negro feeling, how about the suppression of civil liberties, how about the hard remaining core of poverty in one country which has within its reach the abolition of poverty?"—I can only answer with Prospero in *The Tempest,* pointing to the human beast Caliban, " This thing of darkness I acknowledge mine." But in acknowledging it we must fight unceasingly, not with the weapons of class or religious hatred, of conspiracy or of terror, but with anger at injustice and laughter at the hollowness of the stuffed shirts, with compassion for victim and oppressor alike, and with unswerving resolve to understand the nature of the destructive forces that are loose in our world.

When people ask about the American future, I can only answer: there is not just one America—there is the America of privilege and smugness, of lethargy and inequality, of discrimination, of violence, of conformity, of slackness, of corruption; but there is also the America of access to opportunity, of an open society, of the belief in the human potential. These Americas are not outside us. Each of us carries both within him, like two warring kingdoms in the human heart. The future of our culture will be decided in our own hearts and brains.

When Walt Whitman presented a copy of *Leaves of Grass* to his master, Ralph Waldo Emerson, he wrote in it: " Master, I am a man who has perfect faith. Master, we have not come through centuries, caste, heroisms, fables to halt in this land today." As I look toward the future of America and its culture, after all the greatness that we have had, I find myself an enemy of anyone who asks us to halt in this land today.

References

CHAPTER II

1. Guglielmo Ferrero, *The Principles of Power*, trans. Theodore R. Jaeckel (New York: G. P. Putnam's Sons, 1942), p. 22.

2. W. Lloyd Warner and James C. Abegglen, *Big Business Leaders in America* (New York: Harper and Brothers, 1955), p. 220. Permission to quote has been granted by the publisher.

3 Denis W. Brogan, " The End of Illusion," *The Yale Review*, XLVII (December, 1957), 161-162.

4. Brooks Adams, *The Theory of Social Revolutions* (New York: The Macmillan Company, 1914), p. 228.

CHAPTER III

1. Quoted in Hans B. Thorelli, *The Federal Antitrust Policy* (Baltimore: The Johns Hopkins Press, 1955), pp. 335-336.

2. Quoted in Elmer Ellis, *Mr. Dooley's America* (New York: Alfred A. Knopf, 1941), p. 170.

3. Irvin G. Wyllie, *Self-Made Man in America* (New Brunswick: Rutgers University Press, 1954), p. 164.

4. *The Independent*, LIV (April, 1902), 781-788.

5. Herbert Hoover, *Memoirs* (3 vols.; New York: The Macmillan Company, 1952), III (*The Great Depression, 1929-1941*), 97.

6. Paul W. Litchfield, *Industrial Voyage* (Garden City: Doubleday and Company, 1954), p. 287.

7. Quoted in Norman Beasley, *Knudsen* (New York: Whittlesey House, 1947), pp. 283-284. Permission to quote has been granted by McGraw-Hill Book Company.

8. *Time*, LXXI (February 17, 1958), 90.

9. W. Lloyd Warner and James C. Abegglen, *Occupational Mobility in American Business and Industry, 1928-1952* (Minneapolis: University of Minnesota Press, 1955).

10. F. W. Taussig and C. S. Joslyn, *American Business Leaders* (New York: The Macmillan Company, 1932).

11. Quoted in Litchfield, *Industrial Voyage*, p. 130.

101

12. Quoted in Thomas C. Cochran, *Railroad Leaders 1845-1890* (Cambridge: Harvard University Press, 1953), p. 85.

13. David Riesman *et al.* *The Lonely Crowd* (New York: Anchor Books, 1955), p. 308.

14. Peter F. Drucker, *The Practice of Management* (New York: Harper and Brothers, 1954), p. 390.

15. C. H. Buford, "How to Become a Railroad President," *What's New* (November, 1949), 12-13.

16. Quoted in Eugene Staley, ed., *Creating an Industrial Civilization* (New York: Harper and Brothers, 1952), p. 62.

17. Quoted in Herrymon Maurer, *Great Enterprise* (New York: The Macmillan Company, 1955), p. 147.

18. *Ibid.*, p. 147.

19. *Ibid.*, p. 161.

20. Drucker, *The Practice of Management*, p. 389.

21. Quoted in Cochran, *Railroad Leaders*, p. 211.

22. E. A. Ross, *Changing America* (Chautauqua: Chautauqua Press, 1909), p. 104.

23. *Oregon Business Review*, XV (September, 1956), 2.

Biographical Notes

THOMAS C. COCHRAN (Ph. D.) is Professor of History at the University of Pennsylvania. He is an Easterner by birth, educated at New York University and the University of Pensylvania. He was for years editor of the *Journal of Economic History*. He has written extensively in the field of business history; perhaps his best known work is *The Age of Enterprise, A Social History of American Business*. His most recent volume, *The American Business System*, appeared in 1957.

MAX LERNER (Ph. D.) did his undergraduate and law work at Yale and his graduate work at Washington University and the Brookings Institution. Both in the past and in the present, his career mixes active work in journalism with an active academic life. He is a daily columnist with the *New York Post* and Professor of American Civilization at Brandeis University. The most recent of his several volumes, *America as a Civilization*, appeared in 1957.

EDWARD LITTLEJOHN (B. Sc. Econ., A. M.) is a businessman. A native of Australia, he took his undergraduate work at Sydney and at the London School of Economics and his graduate work at Harvard. From 1941 to 1948 he served the Australian government in various capacities in New York and Washington. In 1948 he joined the Burroughs Corporation, where he served as assistant to the president, John Coleman, and as director of public relations. Since 1959 he has been with Standard Oil of New Jersey in New York. In November, 1957, as guest editor for *Public Relations Journal*, he was responsible for a noteworthy special issue on " The American Economy."

RAYMOND C. MILLER (Ph. D), holder of this year's Franklin Lectureship, is Professor of History at Wayne State University. A native of the Middle West, he did his undergraduate work in Kansas and his graduate study at the University of Chicago. In 1950 he was the Lewis Cass Lecturer for the Detroit Historical Society. His volume, *Kilowatts at Work: A History of the Detroit Edison Company*, appeared in 1958.

Edited by Paula Thibault

Set in Linotype Baskerville and Bulmer type faces

Printed on Warren's Olde Style Antique Wove
and bound in Elephant Hide paper

Manufactured in the United States of America